THE BEST OF
THE PROSE POEM:
AN INTERNATIONAL JOURNAL

Edited by Peter Johnson

White Pine Press • Buffalo, New York
Providence College • Providence, Rhode Island

Publication of this volume was made possible
by funding from Providence College.

Book design: Robert Booth

Printed and bound in the United States of America
by McNaugton & Gunn, Inc.

This volume was co-published by
Providence College, Providence, Rhode Island
and
White Pine Press, P.O. Box 236, Buffalo, NY 14201.

Library of Congress Cataloging-in-Publication Data

The best of the prose poem: an international journal
/ edited by Peter Johnson ; forward by Peter Johnson.
        p.   cm.
        ISBN 1-893996-08-5
        1. Poetry   2. Prose poems
        I. Johnson, Peter
        PS8498.28.I34X5613 2000
        863—dc21   00-12694
Library of Congress Control Number: 00-040430

THE PROSE POEM: AN INTERNATIONAL JOURNAL

The Prose Poem: An International Journal is published annually by Providence College. Subscriptions are $8.00 per volume. Checks should be made payable to Providence College and mailed to *The Prose Poem: An International Journal,* English Department, Providence College, Providence, RI 02918.

Editor: Peter Johnson
Assistant Editors: Brian Johnson, Karen Klingon
Advisory Editor: Donald L. Soucy
Contributing Editors: Michael Benedikt, Robert Bly, Russell Edson, Sibyl James, Morton Marcus, Naomi Shihab Nye, Charles Simic.
Staff: Talia Danesi, Kurt Johnson, Janet Masso, Katie Miller, Tom Scalzo
Layout and Design: Robert Booth.
Cover Design: Robert Booth, Peter Johnson.

Manuscripts of no more than three to five poems will be considered only between *December 1* and *March 1* of each reading period. The next reading period begins *December 1, 2001*. Unsolicited work submitted before this date will be returned. Please include a SASE and a two-sentence biographical note with your submission.

All correspondence should be directed to Peter Johnson, *The Prose Poem: An International Journal,* English Department, Providence College, Providence, RI 02918.

The Prose Poem: An International Journal is indexed by the Index of American Periodical Verse (Lanham, Maryland Scarecrow Press) and distributed in the United States by B. DeBoer, Inc., 113 E. Centre Street, Rear, Nutley, New Jersey 07110.

The Prose Poem: An International Journal's website may be found on *Web Del Sol* at http://www.webdelsol.com/tpp. Many thanks to Mike Neff for all of his work.

Table Of Contents

Epilogue

Introduction

In editing *The Best of The Prose Poem: An International Journal*, I feel humble and defensive at the same time. First, I am humbled by my inability to articulate anything close to absolute criteria for my "best of" selections. I have read so many prose poems over the past eight years that I feel as if a large gray eraser is squatting in the hollow of my head. I am not even sure what my criteria are, anymore. Some of my contributors would agree with this perception; they have even written to tell me so. Moreover, after reviewing the past eight volumes, I am sometimes disappointed by poems that we have published, and I wonder how many good ones we let go. Since the publication of *Volume 1* in 1992, I have read just about everything written on the prose poem in English. Has that made me a better editor, or has it encouraged me to look at submissions through a distorted critical lens, trying to pigeonhole poems into generally accepted categories? What a terrible failure, what a laughingstock, is the editor who is unable to recognize and to reward the rare visionary poet who succeeds in breaking all the rules—if indeed there are any rules. Yet in spite of these misgivings, I plan to defend or apologize for whatever criteria I have relied on. Readers of Socrates' *Apology* will remember that the Greek word *apologia* means "a defense," though they will also remember, with the sounds of Socrates' rhetoric ringing in their ears, that sometimes the best defense is a good offense.

And so, blockhead, what were you saying about rules? Are there actually do's and don'ts for writing prose poems? Or even more aggressively: *Is there even such a genre as prose poetry?*

I recognize, of course, the humor in editing a collection in a genre which many intelligent poets and critics do not think exists. To some, I might just as well be editing the galactic correspondences of Mr. Spock. At one Associated Writing Program Conference, a well-known poet approached my exhibitor's table, whereupon I enthusiastically offered him a free copy of *The Prose Poem*. He recoiled as if I were handing him a slimy, horned toad, then smugly pointed out that there was no such genre as prose poetry. "Furthermore," he said, his eyebrows twitching like two oversexed centipedes, "even if there is such a genre called prose poetry, it still isn't *real* poetry." "That's why we call it prose poetry," I responded, arguing that he wouldn't criticize a sonnet for not being a villanelle. He laughed and disappeared into a sea of admirers.

My comparison, of course, was weak, since both sonnets and villanelles do have rules, whereas the most that we can say about prose poetry is that it exhibits certain characteristics. In this sense, its nearest literary cousin is another oxymoronic genre, black humor. Bruce Jay Friedman writes that attempting to define black humor is like trying to define "an elbow or a corned-beef sandwich" (vii.). Much the same can be said about prose poetry. In the first volume of *The Prose Poem: An International Journal*, I argued that "Just as black humor straddles the fine line between comedy and tragedy, so the prose poem plants one foot in prose, the other in poetry, both heels resting precariously on banana peels" (6). The critic wrestling with the prose poem-as-genre assumes the same precarious position. For every definitive statement I make on the genre, I recognize the prescriptive flaw in that statement, so that when pontificating on the prose poem, I feel like one of the Three Stooges, alternately slapping myself in the face with each hand:

"The prose poem has its roots in the aphorism."

"But what about the long prose poems of Baudelaire?"

"But surely all prose poems are fables."

"Then where do you situate the 'poetic prose' written by certain Language poets?"

Take this, take that. Whoof! Bang! . . .

Concerning literary definition in general and prose poetry in particular, Russell Edson, in "Portrait of the Writer as a Fat Man," states, "We are not interested in the usual literary definitions, for we have neither the scholarship nor the ear. We want to write free of debt or obligation to literary form or idea; free even from ourselves, free from our own expectations. . . . There is more truth in the act of writing than in what is written. . ." ("Portrait" 38). Edson's scorn for literary pigeon-holing also appears in a recent statement on genre distinctions. "What name one gives or doesn't give to his or her writing," he says, "is far less important than the work itself" ("Interview" 86). Was Frederich Schlegel right, then, when he argued that "Every poem is a genre in itself" (Monroe 245)? Yet, as many recent critical studies on the prose poem suggest (see our bibliography at the back of this volume), it does seem worthwhile to look at some definitions and characteristics of prose poetry offered by poets and critics.

E. M. Cioran writes, "To embrace a thing by definition, however arbitrary . . . is to reject that thing, to render it insipid and superfluous, to annihilate it" (7). It seems that most prose poets would agree with Cioran. Averse to the crippling, straitjacket mentality associated with definition, they circle the prose poem as if it were a crocodile. Instead of nets, they rely on metaphor, trusting in the analogical slices of our brains, which naturally embrace oxymoron and paradox. In a special issue on the prose poem in the journal *Verse*, Charles Simic states, "Writing a prose poem is a bit like trying to catch a fly in a dark room. The fly probably isn't even there, the fly is inside your head, still, you keep tripping over and bumping into things in hot pursuit. The prose poem is a burst of language following a collision with a large piece of furniture" (7). Simic's comparison captures both the spontaneity and the frustration involved in writing a prose poem. Like Simic, Louis Jenkins is awed by the mystery of composition, but his metaphor seems safer and more homemade. "Think of the prose poem as a box," he writes, "perhaps the lunch box dad brought home from work at night. What's inside? Some waxed paper, a banana peel, half a peanut butter-jelly sandwich. Not so much a hint of how the day has gone perhaps, but the magic for having made a mysterious journey and returned. The dried out pb&j tastier than anything made flesh" (1). And then there's Edson, who compares the prose poem to a "cast-iron aeroplane that can actually fly, mainly because its pilot does not care if it does or not."

Nevertheless, this heavier-than-air prose monstrosity, this cast-iron toy will be seen to be floating over the trees.

It's all done from the cockpit. The joy stick is made of flesh. The pilot sits on an old kitchen chair before a table covered with an oilcloth. The coffee cups and spoons seem to be the controls.

But the pilot is asleep. You are right, this aeroplane seems to fly because its pilot dreams. . . .

("Portrait" 38)

Edson's metaphor and his comment on literary definition are attractive to poets because he champions the unconscious and the personal imagination in its attempt to escape literary and cultural contamination. "There is more truth in the act of writing than in what is written" ("Portrait" 38). Yes! Yet is it possible at this point in time to write in a genre unaware that it really is a genre, or to be ignorant of other established genres that it resembles—in our case, the parable, the fable, the aphorism, the pensée, and so on? "Where do genres come from?" Tzvetan Todorov asks. "Quite simply from other genres. A new genre is always a transformation of an earlier one, or of several; by inversion, by displacement, by combination" (15). Whether or not we agree with Todorov, it's clear that many poets and critics have taken a similar approach to the prose poem. Margueritte Murphy wants to free the prose poem from verse, pointing to the "nonliterary language" of

Baudelaire's *Paris Spleen*, with its "political idioms" and "slang of the streets," both of which thwart the critic's attempt to define prose poetry by "relying on the dominance of poetic functions, such as rhythm or metaphor" (89). She argues that the prose poem "remains formally a prose genre," then adds that prose poetry is ruled, "as all genres are, by tradition, if only to undermine it" (63). Whether or not the prose poem likes it, Murphy suggests, it must subvert those genres to be "other."

Charles Simic also recognizes that the prose poem is a "literary hybrid,"

> an impossible amalgamation of lyric poetry, anecdote, fairy tale, allegory, joke, journal entry, and many other kinds of prose. Prose poems are the culinary equivalent of peasant dishes, like paella and gumbo, which bring together a great variety of ingredients and flavors, and which in the end, thanks to the art of the cook, somehow blend. Except, the parallel is not exact. Prose poetry does not follow a recipe. The dishes it concocts are unpredictable and often vary from poem to poem.
>
> ("A Long Course" 15)

Indeed, any successful description of the genre seems to include this element of unpredictability. When I first began writing prose poems and consciously considering prose poetry as a distinct genre, I thought of the platypus, that lovable yet homely Tasmanian hybrid, but then came to see the weakness of that comparison. The platypus's genetic code is predetermined. It can't all of sudden grow an elephant's trunk out of its backside, that is, unless it ends up in a Russell Edson poem. In contrast, the prose poem's possible transformations are endless.

If there is such a creature as the prose poem, and if its existence depends partly on its ability to plunder the territories of many other like genres, then perhaps we can discuss it in terms of some recognizable tradition and look at the "traditional" prose poem as having certain characteristics. Michael Benedikt, in the introduction to his groundbreaking anthology, *The Prose Poem: An International Anthology* (will some visionary publisher ever reprint this wondrous collection?), provides some general characteristics which continue to be useful. First, Benedikt traces the modern prose poem back to the French Symbolists and to Robert Bly's "Looking for Dragon Smoke," the latter essay explaining the new direction in which American poetry was moving during the 60s and 70s. Then he gives a "working definition" of the prose poem, arguing that it "is a genre of poetry, self-consciously written in prose, and characterized by the intense use of virtually all the devices of poetry, which includes the intense use of devices of verse," except for the line break (47). Finally, he lists what he calls the "special properties" of the prose poem: its "attention to the unconscious, and to its particular logic"; "an accelerated use of colloquial and everyday speech patterns"; "a visionary thrust"; a reliance on humor and wit; and an "enlightened doubtfulness, or hopeful skepticism" (48-50).

Michel Delville, in the only complete study of the American prose poem, *The American Prose Poem: Poetic Form and the Boundaries of Genre*, recognizes the usefulness of Benedikt's "properties" but also points out their indebtedness to the Surrealist tradition because they privilege the unconscious, and thus best describe the prose poetry of writers whom Delville calls "neo-Surrealists," such as Edson and Benedikt himself. An obvious problem occurs because many prose poets are not Surrealists; they may even loathe the movement. Unlike Benedikt, Delville argues that he

> will approach the notion of genre itself as an historical rather than a theoretical category, that is, by drawing inductively on an existing body of contemporary works labeled, marketed or simply received as prose poems, rather than by establishing a prescriptive construct which would precondition [his] attempts to come to the terms with the texts themselves. (9)

We have to look beyond "the existence of generic boundaries as such," Delville writes, "to look for similarities and differences between individual works. As Paul Hernadi writes, 'things may be similar in *different respects*'" (10). And Delville does an excellent job tracing the history of the American prose poem from the influence of James Joyce's "epiphanies," through the short prose of Gertrude Stein, Sherwood Anderson, and Kenneth Patchen, up to the "fabulist" and "deep image" schools, team-taught by Russell Edson, Robert Bly, Michael Benedikt, David Ignatow, Maxine Chernoff, and Charles Simic. Delville also discusses at length the "prose poem" associated with the Language school of poetry—a "poetic prose," which, from my point of view, can be problematic, since many of its practitioners and apologists often disparage the "traditional" prose poem of such fabulators as Edson. The title of Stephen Fredman's excellent study, *Poet's Prose: The Crisis in American Verse*, shows how far some critics will go to avoid the term "prose poetry," which term Fredman writes, "remains redolent with the atmospheric sentiment of French Symbolism" (10). Indeed, the distinctions he makes between the "traditional" prose poem and "poet's prose" allow him to illuminate, in a way Benedikt's "properties" cannot, such texts as William Carlos Williams' *Kora in Hell*, Robert Creeley's *Presences: A Text for Marisol*, John Ashbery's *Three Poems*, and David Antin's "talk poems." By the time we finish Fredman's study, it is difficult to even look at the above works as prose poems. And so, again, we come full circle.

I have provided this overview of recent approaches to the prose poem for two reasons. First, I want to argue that so much critical literature on the prose poem may itself suggest that prose poetry is not only a "real" genre, but that it also has a tradition. Secondly, in terms of my criteria for choosing poems, I must admit that besides all the prose poems and fables and fairy tales and parables and prose fragments I have read over the years, I have been influenced by the above critical approaches to the prose poem. Although they haven't provided me with guidelines, they have created a context from which I must draw, even if I do so unconsciously. To me, literary theory, like philosophy, provides few answers; instead, and perhaps more importantly, it creates an endless internal and external dialogue which forces us to constantly reevaluate our standards. I honestly do not know, nor do I care to know, how this dialectic affects the writer. From reading Robert Bly's "The Prose Poem as an Evolving Form," I am aware of his division of prose poems into fables, poems of illumination, and object poems. From reading Jonathan Monroe's *A Poverty of Objects: The Prose Poem and the Politics of Genre*, I have learned to look at the prose poem from a sociocultural perspective, and Monroe has altered the way I read such writers as Novalis, Baudelaire, and especially Max Jacob and Francis Ponge. And certainly, one of the first major studies of the prose poem in English, *The Prose Poem in France: Theory and Practice*, edited by Mary Ann Caws and Hermine Riffaterre, influenced my original conception of the prose poem-as-genre. But, again, I cannot say how all this reading, along with the correspondence and conversations I have had with other poets on the "nature" of the prose poem, has affected my own writing. I still feel as startled as a newborn kitten by what appears on the page. Even if it stinks. I have come to trust in my imagination as a poet, just as I have come to trust in my judgment as an editor. Write the prose poems, reread the masters of the genre, delve into the critical material, then take a deep breath and open those envelopes, hoping a wee bit of literary competence has been acquired. Certainly, if I look hard enough, I can categorize the prose poems we receive; they will be poems of illumination, or formal prose poems, or object poems. The writers themselves will be neo-Surrealists, or Language poets, or Midwestern raconteurs. But even if these writers self-consciously embrace such schools, I know that most of them never think of these designations when they sit down to write. So I, too, must look at each poem as if it *is* its own genre, and I believe my assistant editors and I have tried to read submissions in this open-minded fashion. That's not to say we don't see common, fatal errors in prose poems. The enemies of any good poem will always be sentimentalism and a morbid self-consciousness. And let's not forget self-indulgence, verbosity. Certainly, I have no desire to create an "us" (prose poets) versus "them" (verse poets) mentality, especially since ninety-five percent of the poets in this volume write in both forms, yet it is frustrating when many contributors, most of them already accomplished verse poets, seduced by the so-called freedom of the prose poem, cavalierly write, "I have read and enjoyed your journal, so I thought I'd dash off a few prose poems for your consumption." To us hardcore prose poets, these writers might just as well be saying, "I thought I'd try brain surgery on myself, drunk and blindfolded." If the free verse poet must be more demanding on herself than the sonneteer, then the prose poet must be merciless. "Too much language chasing too little of an idea" ("Interview" 89), Edson has said, and we nod our heads in agreement, knowing that we reject most submissions because they are overwritten.

All the poems included in *The Best of The Prose Poem: An International Journal* have avoided the above flaws, or, I hope, have succeeded in spite of them. In the introduction to *Volume 1*, I wrote that "I often selected [prose poems] driven by a distinctive voice, a voice demanding attention, one that yelled out, 'Hey, try to ignore my vision if you can'" (6). Whether the prose poets included here have privileged form over content or vice versa, whether they are Surrealists or Language poets, minimalists or maximalists, I probably have chosen their poems for the same reason I made my choices in *Volume 1*. Are my selections more informed now than they were eight years ago? Who knows. Perhaps Edson, again, offers the best answer to all the questions I have raised and have deliberately left unanswered. "The world's a strange place," he tells us, "it helps to think of oneself as a secret agent" (88). Not a bad metaphysics for the prose poet.

At this stage in the journal, it seems appropriate to thank a number of people. First, I thank Providence College for publishing *The Prose Poem: An International Journal*. I have been fortunate to work under a number of intelligent Vice Presidents and Associate Vice Presidents. First, there was Dr. James McGovern, who provided the initial funding for the journal. Next, past Vice President Rev. Thomas McGonigle gave me a course reduction at a time when the journal doubled in terms of workload. Finally, current Vice President Dr. Thomas L. Canavan, an English professor himself, has given both moral and financial support as the journal continues to grow.

I also need to thank my two assistant editors, Karen Klingon and Brian Johnson, who helped me make final selections in the first eight volumes, and who sometimes helped read through the general submissions. Karen, an artist, poet, and children's writer, read for the first four volumes. Her intolerance for affectations kept many a bad poem out of the journal. Brian is, quite simply, one of the best readers of poetry I have met. It has been a pleasure to reprint some of his own prose poems in this volume because he had to give up that privilege when he became an editor. Moreover, there would have been no *Volume 5* if Brian hadn't lugged all the submissions back and forth to me after I broke a vertebra and was housebound. Both he and Karen pulled me away from my Darvocet and reruns of the original *Wild Wild West*. Thanks to Don Soucy, too, an old friend, who took charge of book reviews and some of the proofreading. Also, I must mention Bob Booth, Cathy Walsh, Janet Masso, and all the students who helped in various ways, especially Jean Hopkinson, Chris Macli and Talia Danesi. Finally, I applaud my contributing editors who somehow knew I wouldn't embarrass them.

I could go on and on mentioning all the prose poets who have been supportive over the years, but I'm sure I would leave someone out, so I will end here by offering a final thanks to all of you who have sent us work and money, and who have encouraged me to keep editing this journal.

Please note that we will begin reading for *Volume 10* on December 1, 2001. There will be no volume published next year.

Peter Johnson

Works Cited

Benedikt, Michael. *The Prose Poem: An International Anthology*. New York: Dell, 1976.

Bly, Robert. *Selected Poems*. New York: Harper Collins, 1986.

Caws, Mary Ann, and Hermine Riffaterre, eds. *The Prose Poem in France: Theory and Practice*. New York: Columbia University Press, 1983.

Cioran, E. M. *A Short History of Decay*. Trans. Richard Howard. New York: The Viking Press, 1975.

Delville, Michel. *The American Prose Poem: Poetic Form and the Boundaries of Genre*. Gainesville: University Press of Florida, 1998.

Edson, Russell. "Portrait of the Writer as a Fat Man." In *A Field Guide to Contemporary Poetry and Poetics*. Eds. Stuart Friebert, David Walker, and David Young. Oberlin: Oberlin College Press, 1997: 35-43.

_____. "Interview." In *The Prose Poem: An International Journal*. Vol. 8. Ed. Peter Johnson. Providence: Providence College Press, 1999: 85-100.

Fredman, Stephen. *Poet's Prose: The Crisis in American Verse*. 2nd ed. Cambridge: Cambridge University Press, 1990.

Friedman, Bruce Jay. Foreword to *Black Humor*. New York: Bantam 1965.

Jenkins, Louis. *Nice Fish*. Duluth: Holy Cow! Press, 1995.

Johnson, Peter. "Introduction." *The Prose Poem: An International Journal*. Vol. 1. Providence: Providence College Press, 1992.

Monroe, Jonathan. *A Poverty of Objects: The Prose Poem and the Politics of Genre*. Ithaca, NY: Cornell University Press, 1987.

Murphy, Margueritte. *A Tradition of Subversion: The Prose Poem in English from Wilde to Ashbery*. Amherst: University of Massachusetts Press, 1992.

Simic, Charles. "The Poetry of Village Idiots." *Verse,* Vol. 13, No. 1. (1996): 7-8.

_____. "A Long Course in Miracles." In Peter Johnson. *Pretty Happy!* Fredonia: White Pine Press, 1997: 15-17.

Todorov, Tzvetan. *Genres in Discourse*. Trans. Catherine Porter. Cambridge: Cambridge University Press, 1990.

Kim Addonizio

LAST GIFTS

They were gathered in the room next to the kitchen, where he had his hospital bed cranked up. A writer he had published brought him a long red boa and draped it around his neck; he looked like someone drowning, a small head floating on feathery waves. Someone else brought a pillow stitched with a picture of Elvis, with the words "King of Rock and Roll" across the top. There were red splotches on his arms, and his hand shook slightly when he poured water into the glass on his tray. A poet took a book off the crowded shelves, sat on the edge of the bed and read to him for a while. Someone accidentally stood on the oxygen hose; no one noticed until he began to cough, and there was some consternation, and then relieved laughter and joking. The party grew more animated; people refilled their drinks, and everyone started talking at once. His wife went to the kitchen and brought back a big silver bowl of buttered popcorn and passed it around. For a few moments it seemed as though they had forgotten him. Then someone finished a story, someone else paused to think of the right word, and a silence opened and spread through the brightly lit room. The guests looked at each other; some had tears in their eyes. They turned to the bed, where the sick man sat smiling at them in his red boa, and he knew this was what it would be like when he was gone. And then he was.

—for Al

Robert Alexander

IN THE *SPORTSMAN*

In the Sportsman Restaurant, old photos line the wall on either side of the huge brick fireplace—photos from the turn-of-the-century Grand Marais: old fishing boats, piles of raw lumber and white-pine boards, folks in dark suits and hats. Eating lunch in the cool dark bar, I see a crowd standing on the boardwalk in front of the old Hargrave & Hill general store, looking back across the dirt street at the photographer, who's standing pretty much where the soldier's monument is today. In the group of a dozen or so people, I see a dog that looks like my own— same size, same pattern of black and white, white paws, white muzzle, black ears and face and body. The dog watches the photographer across the street with his large portrait camera. My dog's standing there, what's most amazing, the same quizzical expression on her face—slightly sad, mortal, life all too short—looking across the street, in front of a store that nearly a century ago burned to the ground. . . .

Agha Shahid Ali

DEAR SHAHID,

I am writing to you from your far-off country. Far even from us who live here. Where you no longer are. Everyone carries his address in his pocket so that at least his body will reach home.

Rumors break on their way to us in the city. But word still reaches us from border towns: Men are forced to stand barefoot in snow waters all night. The women are alone inside. Soldiers smash radios and televisions. With bare hands they tear our houses to pieces.

You must have heard Rizwan was killed. Rizwan: Guardian of the Gates of Paradise. Only eighteen years old. Yesterday at Hideout Café (everyone there asks about you), a doctor—who had just that morning treated a 16-year-old boy released from an interrogation center—said: *I want to ask the fortune-tellers: Did anything in his line of Fate reveal that the webs of his hands would be cut with a knife?*

This letter, *insh'Allah,* will reach you, for my brother goes south tomorrow where he shall post it. Here one can't even manage postage stamps. Today I went to the post office. Across the river. Bags and bags—hundreds of canvas bags—all of undelivered mail. By chance I looked down and there on the floor I saw this letter addressed to you. So I am enclosing it. I hope it's from someone you are longing for news of.

Things here are as usual, though we always talk about you. Will you come soon? Waiting for you is like waiting for spring. We are waiting for the almond blossoms. And, if God wills, O! those days of peace when we all were in love and the rain was in our hands wherever we met.

Jack Anderson

MORAL DISCOURSE

There were these three prisoners. All three had heads on their shoulders. The fact that they were prisoners didn't mean they were stupid. Indeed, they had a serious talk. At least, two of them did. The third mostly kept his mouth shut while the others spoke about him. He was widely held to be innocent, the victim of injustice and, what's more, was said to be some sort of wise man.

That riled the first one, who grumbled, "If you're so smart, why didn't you do something to get us out of this?"

But the second one interrupted, "Well, we did do what they say we did. Let's face it: we deserve this, we really can't complain. So why whine? But this guy's different. He ought to complain. Yet he's taking it like a man."

This conversation went on while all three were dying on crosses. They pondered what might have been and what could be; they mulled over innocence, guilt, and responsibility while nails were tearing into their flesh.

At least, that's what Luke says. But Luke, or whoever wrote those words, never says anything about pain. Surely, there must have been pain, excruciating pain. Yet Luke overlooks it. Instead, he focuses upon moral issues, philosophical problems, sober (if occasionally grumpy) discourse. This is how he views the scene. Others might see it otherwise.

For instance, when Jesus tells the second prisoner, "Today shalt thou be with me in paradise," someone might wonder why he didn't make that same promise to the first guy who did, after all, raise a genuinely provocative issue and hadn't bothered with flattery. But another observer here might be conscious only of the pain. And someone else might ask, "In such a situation, what's the point of discussing anything?"

Jack Anderson

ANGELS

Essentially, they are alike. And no one has ever seen one, for there is nothing there to see.

Those who think they see them see only their trappings: their garments, perhaps, or their passing expressions, but never their actual features: they have none. Yet they do exist, they are real.

Still, all we know of them is through appearances, the likenesses they don to bring their messages to us. They come here solely to deliver their messages. That is the reason for their being. They are their messages. And those messages are urgent, always.

That is why they put on guises, why they work their way into our consciousness. That is why they come as someone strange but interesting, someone who attracts your attention, someone tugging at your sleeve, someone with flashing eyes, someone making you wonder so much that you are caught in a spell and you attend to the message.

Now only the message remains, while its bearer, however intriguing or alluring, disappears. You find yourself alone, totally alone, bearing the weight of these tidings: inexplicable, overwhelming, unbelievable, to be believed.

Nin Andrews

THE OBSESSION

Occasionally the sailor suspects a woman swims nude beneath his ship, though when he dives into the water, he sees only white jellyfish opening and closing like umbrellas. He is reminded of the time when he was a boy and imagined ordinary stones were gems, lovely enough to win the heart of the girl next door. But he never reached to pick one up. Instead he decided the girl would never like him. The more he thought about her not liking him, the more he grew to despise her and her adolescent beauty. The more he despised her, the more he wanted to see her, to follow her, to sit just behind her, and never let her out of his sight. That was the beginning of the obsession. Evenings he stayed up late, peeking through his Venetian blinds, hoping to catch a glimpse of her in her pink striped pajamas. Every weeknight she stretched out on the lime green carpet in her living room and did her homework in front of the flickering TV. The boy began to believe that if he did not watch her, she might not do her homework. Then she might do poorly in school and be mocked, and he would have to protect her. What if he didn't know how? Better to be sure she did her work. But the more he stared at her, the more beautiful she became, the more her skin softened, and the silk of her hair awakened him from his dreams. He grew convinced his eyes gave off a kind of glow that polished the girl, like an apple, that she could never have been as lovely if he had not looked at her so intensely. He even thought his staring might have been making her breasts grow, just as the sun's heat caused fruit to ripen. That's when he realized her beauty was a kind of death wish. Like a mirage, he thought. A mirage of an oasis in the Sahara, something that could never satisfy his thirst. No wonder years later he still saw her breasts in the middle of the sea. No wonder he hated her.

Nin Andrews

THE SUMMER MY SISTER TURNED FOURTEEN,

July turned so sweltering, the pond shriveled into a mud puddle, and the polliwogs wriggled in the creek mud where cats swatted them out with their claws. Jimmy took up helping her in the vegetable garden, sinking in the tomato sticks and weeding the okra and beans and things. Nights he'd be waiting for her in the old tire swing. My sister would beg me to go out back with her and Jimmy while they'd sit side by side, the hairs on their arms almost touching, staring at ants crawling around a bucket rim or peeling labels off a pop bottle while listening to the bullfrogs and katydids. Sometimes the rain smell hung close as sweat, and heat lightning lit up the air where bats swooped overhead. I'd get so bored, I'd say something silly to try to break the silence, but it seemed like sadness was always hovering over them like a stranded angel or some kind of song I never could get the hang of, no matter how hard I listened or how long they waited.

Nin Andrews

IN GRANDMA'S BATHROOM

Centipedes scurried up the stone wall, squeezing into the cracks. I'd stare into her broken mirror and at the row of empty cologne bottles. Her toilet never stopped running. Grandma would come in and rattle the handle, take the top off the tank, pull the black ball in the back, saying I wasn't supposed to be using the facilities in there anyhow. As if her huge, ancient behind made the pink porcelain seat unfit for my bony young one. One time Grandma sat on the toilet seat and broke it. Another time I came in and saw her, wrinkled and wet, rising up like a genie out of a bottle. There was so much of her, I couldn't stop staring and wondering how it all fit in one tub, on one set of bones. She dried off all that body with one small towel, saying, "Look here, Honey Child, don't you be slipping in here again, hear?"

Rane Arroyo

LUCKY, THE LATIN LOVER OF LOMBARD, ILLINOIS

> I come into being/through my own magic.
> —*The Bhagavad-Gita*

I slept with white lovers in the cul-de-sac suburbs who in the end just wanted me to say, "Caramba, Lucy" or "de plane, de plane." No zoot suit for this rico suave English major who claimed Sal Mineo's tragedy in *Rebel Without A Cause* as private property. *Home* was an island of smells: sofrito, carne asada, "Spanish" rice. We learned to love French fries, Boston baked beans, Buffalo wings. In the locker room at the pool, men praised my "full" tan but to me they were just ghosts in steam. Dressed, I was a spy among the mall people. I ironed my hair as friends permed theirs. The timing, it's about time. I had to take a foreign language class but I said I was already in honors English. I never dreamt of the wild west, or of mountain farms in Puerto Rico, but of the red city burning only miles from me. I'd take trains and disappear only to reappear in the suburbs as a messenger: *innocence isn't forever, amigos*. Our bodies were the wrong bridges of escape and so we drove up and down Main Street, like the dizzy sperm of astronauts circling the familiarized planet. One by one, I would drop off my friends at their inevitably white-colored homes. Finally, when alone, as a ritual between the road and me, I'd blast *Black Magic Woman*. Sometimes I would cruise around, wave at the transvestites hiding off the Lilac Trail. For my 25th Class Reunion I was reported as "missing." So typical—as if their reality is the only one. I wasn't missing at all or how else could you find me in your bed tonight?

Rose Ausländer

PRIVACY

Sometimes I wish to be left alone and undisturbed. But that's impossible: street noise and the voices of neighbors live in my room. If I open the window, gnats, flies, moths, sparrows fly in, sometimes even an elf or an angel. Each wants something from me: a little blood, the scent of my skin, a morsel of food, a malicious prank, a soft-spoken hallelujah. You'd like to give each their due, but you have to give yourself your due as well, hear your own voice, leave off the pious prayers, be able to curse everything. This happiness is seldom given.

Translated from the German
by **Gary Sea**

Rose Ausländer

PROGRESS

I live on the first floor of the first house in the first street of this place.
This place is an island. It has only one street. The street has only one
house. The house has only one floor. I am the only tenant. I live on fruit
and fish. On salty sea air, on sun and rain. On thoughts and dreams. My
friends are scattered throughout the world. We write to each other by
the bottle-post. I don't know the name of my island. Now and then, a
bottle is washed onto the beach. That's how I learn about what's going
on in the world, about the great progress being made in all professions.
Wars and murders multiply tenfold. Everyone is proud of their war, of
their victory, yes, even of their defeat.

Translated from the German
by **Gary Sea**

Ruth Behar

POEM XXXV

I thought I would never hear a bird sing again. I thought the trees would forget how to grow leaves. The winter was too long. Too silent. The house fell dark and I could no longer tell the day from the night. I was certain our love had died. I wept and wept. I filled a box with my tears. They shone like pearls that once knew how to swim in the ocean.

Today all the windows are open. Since dawn the birds have been singing deliriously. The trees have turned crazy green. I can smell the flowers in my garden yielding their honey to the bees.

I never wanted a garden—

I did not plant the flowers, I do not know the names of the birds or the trees, yet their wild pleasure is not withheld from me.

How fortunate is the world that it does not depend on my will. How fortunate am I that you keep watering the stem of our love, even when it withers, even when it has nothing to give.

Michael Benedikt

THE TOYMAKER GLOOMY BUT THEN AGAIN SOMETIMES HAPPY

(1) How can a person practically drowning in the seas of circumstance, and beneath wave after wave of our usual, daily, dirty, diurnal dreck, possibly attempt to engage full-time in the production of Magical Objects? That is, I think, a relatively simple question which perhaps virtually every person who prides himself on being both a serious craftsperson and a good citizen of our ordinary, everyday world must ask himself or herself every now and then. Good heavens!—just try waking up first thing in the morning with a few nice, clear Visions of Bliss in your head, and then try perambulating just a few blocks beyond the relative safety and calm of your own house or apartment—and just see how long your own otherwise probably quite cheery, creative, early-morning attitude survives even *that* little stroll into madness and disorder! Yes, if only as a form of minor mental exercise, just try calculating the exact effect that your own very first everyday encounters with the external world and the people in it exert upon you and your own, otherwise probably rather optimistic, fresh-as-a-daisy, early-morning disposition—and see then whether you really feel like going around all day long thinking playful, creative thoughts, chuckling pleasantly to yourself, and generally smiling and laughing! (2) I don't know how you feel about it, but for years and years, from the point of view of a person practicing my own, would-be benignly optimistic profession—that of a struggling manufacturer of colorful and sometimes even relatively amusing toys—I've felt that this constant placing of myself into bad moods by the conventional world, practically amounts to theft! Theft of my good moods, theft of my creative, inventive capacities—theft, even, of my precious peace-of-mind! Don't you, yourself, think that us serious craftspeople spend a whole lot more time than we should have to, defending ourselves against the incursions of a virtual slew of tedious mentalities, seemingly intent on slipping themselves into our mental or even actual billfolds? (3) Still, we press on! As a devoted Toymaker, for example, I for one know that I must! The children, after all, want to be entertained! The public is practically crying out for novelty! (4) And besides, there's at least one additional reason for those of us who happen to be Toymakers, for example, to press on: the fact is that Toymakers, too, sometimes get

miserably bored! And so, occasionally (sometimes when we least ex-pect it!), we feel the sudden urge to try to produce, in counter-response, a pretty doll with eyes sharp and bright enough to light up the world; or, sometimes, a stuffed teddy-bear which sings whimsical tunes—and which, every now & then, sometimes even dances. . . .

Aloysius Bertrand

VIOL DA GAMBA

> He recognized, without doubt, the pale visage of his
> dear friend Jean-Gaspard Debureau, the best clown
> in the Funambule Theater. As he stared at it, an
> expression of indescribable malice and amusement
> rose on his face.
>
> —Theophile Gautier, Onuphrius

> My good friend Pierrot
> Lend me your quill
> So I can write a word or two
> Under the light of the moon.
> My candle's gone out.
> There's not a light in the house.
> For the love of God, Pierrot,
> Open your door.
>
> —Popular Song

The choirmaster had just begun interrogating his viola, drawing his bow across its humming body, when it answered him with jeers and catcalls more often heard at a burlesque show. It seemed that a definite indigestion from too much exposure to slapstick had lodged in its belly.

First, Barbara, the chaperone, bawled out that idiot Pierrot, that stupendous klutz, for dropping the box containing Mr. Cassandre's wig. Powder was flying all over the place.

Mr. Cassandre picked up his wig with a crushed look on his face, and Harlequin gave the blockhead a swift kick in the ass. Colombine laughed so hard she had to wipe a tear from her eye. And Pierrot let loose a white-painted clown's grin that stretched from ear to ear.

But, not long after this, beneath a full moon, Harlequin begged his friend Pierrot to unlock his door so he could get something to relight his candle. The old man stood there, whining at the door even though the bastard had made off with his young lady, not to mention his money.

"The devil take Job Hans, that good-for-nothing lute-maker, who sold me this bowstring!" the choirmaster exclaimed as he placed the dusty viola back in its dusty case. The string had broken.

Translated from the French
by Gian Lombardo

Robert Bly

WARNING TO THE READER

Sometimes farm granaries become especially beautiful when all the oats or wheat are gone, and wind has swept the rough floor clean. Standing inside, we see around us, coming in through the cracks between shrunken wall boards, bands or strips of sunlight. So in a poem about imprisonment, one sees a little light.

But how many birds have died trapped in these granaries. The bird, seeing freedom in the light, flutters up the walls and falls back again and again. The way out is where the rats enter and leave; but the rat's hole is low to the floor. Writers, be careful then by showing the sunlight on the walls not to promise the anxious and panicky blackbirds a way out!

I say to the reader, beware. Readers who love poems of light may sit hunched in the corner with nothing in their gizzards for four days, light failing, the eyes glazed . . .

They may end as a mound of feathers and a skull on the open boardwood floor . . .

Robert Bly

AN OYSTER SHELL

The shell is scarred, as if it were a rushing river bottom, scratched by the great trees being carried down. Sometimes its whitish calcium has been folded over itself, as when the molten rock flows out; so something is still angry.

When we turn it over, we feel that the shell on the inside is more secretive, more finished, more human. Our fingers feel the smooth inside and know of blueberries, earned pleasure, the sweet loneliness of the old man late at night, when angels keep looking for him in the early dawn, calling across the snow-covered fields.

Michael Bowden

BEATNIKS

Red neon staggers through tubes, endlessly leaving arrows at the
entrance to the Wigwam Motel. Indicating vacancies. Outside the
secondhand store, a Free Box bloated on mysteries and a romance in
hardback. A slightly-used treatise on Being open to a random page on
the scuffed linoleum. Now some cat with a black goatee mews his
poem into a pool of shadows, looking for a mate or maybe just his
bongos. Trumpeting the advent of a viral melancholy. Was it Ginsberg
who first spotted the dead poets tramping back into ordinary streets—
Whitman at the market, bagging blue plums? Cupping each in his palm
a long moment, enjoying the skin's smooth coolness? So perhaps that is
Rimbaud emerging from the flophouse alley, disappearing into the hiss-
ing doors of the Central bus. A rucksack thrown over his shoulder. A
halo gouged into his scalp by some barber college novice. And there's
Follain climbing down a manhole ladder to inspect a broken main. The
past is a Class One narcotic. Memory, its dimebag. Its proactive agent.
Everyone knows where to cop a fix. Everyone's loaded with stories.
Remember the toyshop owner who bought a monkey to promote his
store? He unlocked the doors one morning to find Jocko in a riot of torn
boxes and dolls, his jaunty beret askew. A stacked cheerleader in one
paw, his penis in the other. Which explains why the green parrot in the
barbershop window munched a black gumball, watching, unable for a
moment to imitate the real speech of men.

Michael Bowden

IF YOU'RE THERE PICK UP

The voice wanted to be a Buddha. Or at least some small-time denomination's minister, fresh out of Bible School. A wide grin and some white teeth the gospel could pour through. But the hyperthyroid eyes of the little stained-glass Christ embarrassed it. So the voice considered becoming the frycook in his paper hat wailing teen anthems on air guitar, peeling back the layers of an onion. Preparing a stew. Or a moth banking out of darkness as the diner's lights buzz on. A small voice. A soft voice. The voice was pretty sure it wasn't a waitress shouting *ham and eggs*, or a burly driver inscribed with blue tattoos, but it tried anyway. It paid its bill and left a nice tip and paused at the shoeshine stand to talk about the weather. So now this mummy in a bad wig and sunglasses appears in the alley, walking her dog. The voice gets this feeling. Something's ready to reveal itself. Thinks twice about it. Doesn't. Instead, the dog barks at the power lines or sprawled trash cans or the clouds or the yellow dervish of leaves. Who knows what the hell the dog barks at, the way it cranks its neck and twists its face and growls at everything. The voice figures why not? Barks too. Barks until it's blue in the face. Until its jaws ache. The voice that wanted to be a Buddha.

John Bradley

THE ACCIDENT

Spud, that was her name. It said so in black ink on the strip of adhesive tape stuck to the front of her pink and white checked shirt. Spud. I had just rolled over a little girl named Spud.

I was backing out the car, this old Sportabout wagon. The car picked up speed, the brakes couldn't slow it down, and the back window was so fogged I couldn't see anything. The car kept going faster and I did it. I rolled over something. It felt like squash, something starting to rot. Then the car stopped.

He came running up to the car, this man with the little girl in his arms. He looked Japanese, but I wasn't sure. He said nothing, not a word, but he had this look on his face. He wanted to cry and he wanted to kill me. I don't blame him.

He brought the girl to the driver's door. But I wouldn't open it. I reached back to the door behind me, unlocking it. I didn't want him to place the girl in my lap. No, anything but that.

That's when I saw her name. He placed her on the back seat. And I saw it. Spud, it said. She was blond, five or six years old. Maybe this man had adopted her, or maybe he was simply looking out for her today.

In his hand, I could see he held something. Something for the little girl? No, a can of mace. He sprayed me in the face. I knew he had to.

John Bradley

MEMO TO ARIADNE

I'm going to need a change of address, a change of clothes, a motion that's a cross between a shamble, a dodge, and a feint. I'm going to need avuncular bread, homunculus bread, narcissistic bread. I'll need nude photographs of Cindy Crawford and James Dean and Walt Whitman dusted with arsenic. I'm going to need a recipe for a lightning: how much insomnia, how much caffeine, how much flea powder. I know I'm going to need the phone number of someone with the last name of Salt. I'm going to need a way out, a way in, a way back, a way forward, a way to rest along the long way. I'm going to need a book with the caption *Morning is always the center* underneath a colored illustration of an American Indian. I'll need a used Buick with a radio that plays the soundtrack of that Jean Cocteau movie where he's listening to the car radio. I'll need a map of Dixon, Illinois, egg-yolk stains at the bottom right. I'm going to need railroad brandy, hummingbird brandy, clairvoyant brandy. I know I'm going to need a spare prostate. I'll need a copy of the Zapruder film soaked in Visine. I'll need the dental records of Amelia Earhart. I'll need a guarantee of amnesty, a plea for clemency, a pardon for unforeseen acts of malice and mercy. I'm going to need a song with the refrain: *Morning is always the center.* I'll need amniotic samples, a disinterested party, a parry, an opening, a counterclockwise password, an alibi, an operator, a distressed identity, a passport, Swiss bank account, bilingual inoculations, an antidote to the official antidote. I know I'm going to need a portapotty. Don't forget a pair of plague gloves. When you see me at the market beside the paprika stand, tap the side of your nose three times.

Joel Brouwer

TUMOR

I lift your scalp like the lid on a pot of stew and firk the fucker out. I've wondered for weeks which color it really was: the yellow glow on the MRI, the encyclopedia diagram's green pecan, the tiny blue crab from my dreams? You were no help. You slept and slept. I quizzed interns over cafeteria trays: *Red like cherry Jello-O? Darker, like these beets?* Sometimes I imagined it earthworm pink, sometimes grey from all the brain it ate. Now here it is at last: white as an empty ledger. Wake up, you bastard. I can't write this alone.

Joel Brouwer

MARKED

God marked Cain so we would know to curse him, but who pushed the
teapot from the pantry shelf and cut Francine's cheek? And why? The
scar glows white when she's cold: a rice grain in a dish of milk. In
Egypt death passed over doors dabbed with lamb's blood, but in Poland
stopped at each chalked with a star. The pencil salesman's son hides
upstairs, painting the encyclopedia's pages white. His father's shadow
pours into the room like ink into water: *You have to make a mark upon
the world!* The kid dips his brush, says *OK, hold still.*

Christopher Buckley

IGNIS FATUUS

Swamp glow of the Milky Way, platters of dust, arms coiled around the galactic hub like fiery streamers in a black wind—unaccountable, too many stars ever to be of use.

Aren't stars beside the point—starlight, finally, so suburban? Is it still enough to be clever, allusive, like some minor movie star, collar of his black jacket turned up, smoking, overlooking the harbor lights in Denmark? Can you settle for approximations—glittering or not—with the little you have left to offer?

And it's nothing to say that the clouds sometimes climb like roses over the trellis of the blue. A wind insists against clusters of bottle brush and bougainvillea—like renegade clouds, white grocery bags scuttle along the sidewalks, up hill, suspended and darting in the alleyways. Each November galaxies of dry leaves and bracts spin away.

50 now, and never have you discussed rain so reverently . . . there's no doubt—you're going to die. This is no longer some distant city off in the low analogical hills, a theorem you will never have to prove. The scientists have shown that everything returns to something—dust to . . . star dust, of course, so literal, remote, so cold.

Whatever it was I used to think I believed about reincarnation, I have forgotten. I only remember that, for a time, art sustained some vague apotheosis beyond our breath—Velazquez, for instance, standing there, looking out from Las Meniñas, as if he knew. When he was made a Knight of the Court—that blood cross, that star, on his tunic, over his heart, signified that he could move among such shining society. And his painting, well, a brilliant means, not a source burning in and of itself.

My father believed he had been Velazquez, or perhaps the Spanish king who hired him. He must have missed those portraits in the background, hazy, fading in the mirror. And later, how could he have overlooked Christ foreshortened by Mantegna—the grey sticks of his feet poking out the canvas at us? Or Caravaggio—prescient as light—his own head hung in the hand of David, offered to the dark—at 32, his own tired, moon-dead eyes?

So how is the spirit grounded, ground down to stellar gravel or settled dust? The wind moves through the oat grass, the star thistle, its purple heart, its silver points, its pain. Pythagoras proclaimed everything could be solved by numbers. By conforming to the arithmetic of the stars, we could escape the cycle of rebirth—the universe just an algorithm of notes, monochord, string and riffs of light vibrating from spirit at one bright end and blood-dull earth at the other.

In Babylon they catalogued 1,022 stars on a thin celestial globe, a surface which equaled the boundary of heaven—rotation of moon and stars the only dim points to show where they were heading on earth. The world barely spinning then. . . .

Beeswax sky, flame above the sinking edge of space . . . once I could have been found sitting creek-side, cataracts sending up a mist burning at the edge of dawn, content tossing pebbles in a pool, all the time in the world in the relay of ripples. . . . Yet, when I think about it, I never saw angels sauntering through the foothills with timpani or flutes, no one playing "Holiday for Strings"—only the blue rondo of water falling through water, no annotations in the paraffin sky.

The closest I ever came was at 15, surfing Miramar Point on a head-high swell. Salt water and blood rumbling with the breakers, crouched in a glassy tube, cutting back across the lip of the wave to stall and shoot through the curl again for the synergy of atoms and flying space—which is surely the singular reason I was there, though I could not have said it then as I calmly released myself to the cold seconds burning by, to that point where I felt the electron click of blue and yellow light at my fingertips flash out above the salt static and the froth, to burst clear, breathing where light was my only future, and not all that far removed.

Lynne Burris Butler

LUCY Z

Sister, they called her, until she went to school and Teacher said that wasn't a name, what was her name? And she had none, so she named herself Lucy Z. No daddy either except the one who disappeared and the other Mama sent away. But she still had Lloyd and George Ward and Baby Don who all became railroad men, who rode the tracks way out west. So she bought herself a ticket out of that old turtle of a town and went to Memphis, oh southern girl of pecan pies and a good fur wrap, and she studied nursing and got a taste for more, then flew away to California where she met Mary Pickford who gave her a vase of glazed grey porcelain and she had a lover who bought her everything, rings, a belt with silver conches, and begged her to marry him, to move to Nebraska or somewhere like that, but of course she wouldn't which is why she gave me the belt saying, "Oh, it's just something." And she bought Waterford crystal at an antique auction, pieces so fine we'd look for years and never find another and she'd say, "Let's have a toddy for the body," before dinner on her brilliant Chinese plates. "I wouldn't trust a woman whose dishes all match," she taught me. And she loved my husband and adored my son and when they were in the room, I'd disappear one two three into the trick trunk of the unimportant, the insignificant to Lucy Z who had made herself a woman of style.

Chambers / Federman

A LITTLE REQUEST

In the long run, in the scheme of things, what kinds of things do you want a woman to do for you? he asked.

And I replied, as things stand now, with the old bones weeping, and the muscles creaking, I would like a woman to kneel before me and untie my shoelaces.

Maxine Chernoff

THE SOUND

—I hate it when we have sex and you make that sound.

—What sound?

—The sound you make when you're about to have orgasm.

—What sound do you mean?

—I can't describe it. It sounds like no other sound you ever make.

—But why do you hate it?

—It scares me.

—Why would it scare you?

—I guess it's because we're at an intimate moment, and you make an unfamiliar sound.

—It must be my intimate-moment sound.

—But it doesn't sound intimate. It sounds . . . well . . . brutal.

—I make a brutal sound?

—Yes, I think that's how I'd describe it.

—Make the sound for me.

—I can't.

—Of course you can. You remember it, don't you?

—I'm embarrassed to make it.

—You're not embarrassed to tell me, but you're embarrassed to make it?

—Right.

—Just try.

—All right. It's something like "Yowwwww-oh-woe-woe."

—And that sounds brutal to you?

—It does.

—It sounds to me like I'm very happy.

—It doesn't sound happy to me.

—What sound would you like me to make?

—I don't have an alternative in mind. I just thought I'd tell you that the sound you make, well, it brings me out of the moment. Sex ends for me when I hear that sound.

—That's good, isn't it?

—Why is it good?

—Because you know I've had an orgasm when you hear it.

—But what if I want to do something more to you?

—More? We've both finished by then. What more would we do?

—What if I still want to kiss you and you're making that sound?

—Well, I guess you could try and see.

—Should I try now?

—Why do you think I want you to kiss me when you can't stand the sound I make at my most vulnerable moment?

—I didn't mean I couldn't stand it. I just meant it's distracting.

—Maybe you should gag me.

—Then you'd make the sound but it would be even worse.

—Why would it be worse?

—It would sound all muffled and sad, like the voice of someone locked inside of a trunk.

—So, you'd rather I sound brutal than all muffled and sad?

—I guess so.

—You must really love me then.

Maxine Chernoff

HEAVENLY BODIES

—When is that huge meteor scheduled to hit Earth?

—I heard something about 2035.

—You mean in thirty-seven years the world might end?

—The world wouldn't end.

—If a meteor of that size hits Earth, we'll be destroyed.

—We might be destroyed, but there'd still be a world.

—Do you mean a universe?

—I guess that's what I mean.

—How will there be a universe if we're not there to form the concept?

—Do you think we're so important that the whole universe can't exist if we don't? What was here before we were born?

—History was here.

—That's exactly it. We're simply a part of it all, like a whorl in a tree trunk.

—Why didn't you say a grain of sand on a beach?

—Okay, a grain of sand on a beach.

—How can someone who knows so much about the universe be persuaded to use a cliché?

—Death is a cliché.

—What do you mean?

—It's given to us, and we can do nothing to change it.

—But you're saying our own deaths don't matter. Not now. Not in thirty years, not if the universe gets destroyed.

—Exactly.

—So what should we do?

—About what?

—What should we do to prevent the meteor from destroying us?

—I guess we could intercept it.

—Who, you and me?

—The government.

—I knew it.

—Knew what?

—You're some kind of hired assassin.

—What do you mean?

—You're hired by the government to make me think I don't matter, not even if I die.

—How does that make me an assassin?

—It's conceptual. You erase me with your thoughts.

—So maybe I'm more of an artist than an assassin.

—How much do they pay you?

—Who?

—The government.

—Why would the government hire me to convince you of anything? Are either of us so important?

—Here you go again. You just won't admit it.

—Admit what?

—That when we die the universe will perish.

—Okay. When we die the universe will perish. Does that make you feel better?

—Yes, momentarily.

Michael Chitwood

PRACTICUM

One-eyed Jack is discussing theory with the barber. The barber
has nicked Jack's ear.

"In theory, that shouldn't have happened," says the barber, tapping
his glass-covered diploma from barber's school.

"That's the trouble with theories," Jack says, "they don't take into
account the blood."

Jack winks at the boy waiting to get his cut. Jack was a winker long
before he got his eye put out in a fight over a card game.

"Just a friendly game," Jack had said to the others when they caught
him cheating. "That's the trouble with some people," Jack says to the
barber and the boy, "they don't know the difference between a game
and real life—between theory and the hard facts."

The hard fact was the toe of a steel-toed boot. Each time Jack
winks, the boy disappears.

David Citino

THE LAND OF LIARS

> A survey of Italians said 70% had confessed
> to telling between 5 and 10 lies every day.
> —Reuters

In the land of Pinocchio, where even wood can come to life at a magic
word or two, up and down both coasts, from the Alps to Milan, Pisa to
Bologna to Venice and Rome, even in Assisi, especially at the Vatican,
around Naples, throughout Calabria and Sicily of course, noses are grow-
ing. Two-thirds are women who lie in love. *There was never anyone
but you. He wasn't the man you are. None of the others meant a
thing to me. My God you are so big you are killing me. O Christ! O
Jesus! Of course I did. How can you ask that? It's never been that
good before. I've never said those words before.* Men are more
likely to lie on the job. *Not a problem. It's been taken care of. Yes I
know all about that. It's in the mail. It's not my fault. That's not my
responsibility. But I told you about it. I told him just what you told
me. You never told me that. She was begging me for it.* 27% lie to
cover up errors. *God, if you grant me this I'll never ask another
favor. I'll go to church every day. I'll stop doing . . . you know
what.* 42% lie to avoid conflict. *How nice to see you. I haven't told a
soul. Of course I've forgiven you. I'll miss you more than I can say.*
21% lie for the good of someone else. *This is better than my mother
makes it. Actually I prefer my pasta limp and soft, my wine sweet as
candy. That looks great on you. I was just thinking about you. I
swear on my mother's grave. I can't live without you. I'll never lie
to you. I've never lied to you before. I have lied to you before but
this is the gospel truth. Everything I've said is true, essentially.*

Killarney Clary

Clear of oak groves, sunrise stretched a thin reach deep into the chamber, tripping the setting of fires on hilltops: signals relayed to the quarters. A day to plant or hunt, enter women or agreements.

Night skies were laid on fields in perfect orientation before the plates opened, wandered, collided; they continue and will. There is so much to take into account. It may be impossible to choose for myself; all pleasures might hand me loneliness.

I'll find the dark room, tip the white table to catch a shaft bent by a mirror, shot through a pin hole, and I'll watch the ocean upside down. Foam churns at the edge of a vision. It is time to do something in particular.

Killarney Clary

Early radios talk about traffic and weather as if they vary. People phone in with opinions on the metro-rail and stories of most embarrassing moments, and it's slow through the interchange until I glide up onto the ten heading west. I dreamt Russ came to me scared, said he couldn't stop the rainstorm in his mouth.

In another sleep he was a wizard with crescents and stars on a tall hat; this afternoon at lunch he tells me we are made of waves and there is no time. Before we meet again I will forget his face; I will reassign meanings to what we've said.

I stand in the yard tonight; the reflection of the full moon scribbles on the surface of the tea I drink. Instead of figuring it, I watch the figuring; I catch my desire to have it still. Maybe there isn't any code to break.

Mark Cunningham

HAY

Every time, *almost* every time I put a biscuit of shredded wheat, the big ones that come in four or six to a package, into a bowl and pour milk on it, I watch the milk filter through the brittle chunk and think of a bale of hay. Lion's-mane-tan. In a stubble field. Whenever I see a bale of hay I feel the urge to bite into it, feel its dry scour, slightly sweet. I could eat the cows that eat the hay but I don't like meat so I think of big swirled cinnamon rolls, or remember that when I die my body might crumple into soil that feeds the grass that becomes hay: that's a difference between me and hay, I'll never know what becomes of my body after I'm dead, I'm always *before*; but hay is *after,* hay isn't hay until it's dead grass. Heraclitus was right, fire drives all things. No wonder Monet painted hay, stack after stack in fields of snow, in dry morning sun, in late afternoon slant, shine soaking into haystacks and cathedrals, over and over, before he moved to the pond, the clouds, all things moving, in flux. I like the haystacks best in late summer, noon glare already starting to cool, warmth shrinking from general to specific, I like the hay where a cricket calls, my hair in the sun. Po Chu-i was glad to go bald, it was a weight, literally, off his mind, he could see why Buddhist monks shaved their heads before starting on the path away from all the things that were burning, burning, but the only part of growing old I regret is that my hair is thinning, in a year or two I'll become one of those men who sweep a long swath over their bare scalp, fooling no one. Still, I'll be able to feel the sun in my hair a little longer, warm and close, the way it must linger in haystacks those mild afternoons after the first frost. That's why those men comb their hair that way. I'm sure of it.

Craig Czury

BUT THESE BOYS TODAY

> In the ocean, a man dissolves like a bar of salt.
> And the water doesn't know it.
> > —Pablo Neruda

don't dissolve . . . not yet. Maybe not yet for another few years—or the next wave. Maybe not until they get home. I can't tell at what age the men here stop becoming boys. Wave after wave pounds them face down and under—whitewash of last breath and sprawled-out hair. I can't tell, when there's so much clowning around, if the sea really loves these boys— pulling their underpants down below their hinnies and roaring—or if there's something churning and sadistic going on. Of course only a gringo would think this. In the ocean angry sex and gentle sex are the same wave. It's all in how you breathe and let go of your bowels.

When these boys walk away they're exhausted, completely filled and emptied. And they are no longer laughing. Maybe they're no longer boys! One thing for sure, when an angry man has sex with the sea . . . wave after wave . . . it's not the sea who becomes the boy.

Philip Dacey

PSALM FOR FAY

> "Dad, my dream is to marry a matador in
> Ireland and have a big Jewish wedding."

Behold, beside the waters of the River Liffey, I will give my daughter away as I wave a red cape at the groom.

Whereupon shall a bull lie down like a lamb amongst us, under the four-cornered indoor sky of our silken chuppah, his sweet and warm breath more powerful, yea, more appealing than incense, and his eyes as black as the blood pudding served for breakfast in the modest and welcoming homes of Westport, County Mayo.

Verily, the ghost of Fay's great-grandfather Owen McGinn, having come directly from his childhood home and current haunt, Cavan, and looking like Yahweh Himself, will usher astonished guests to their seats.

For I have seen the guest list, Lord, and it includes Leopold Bloom, who shall sing a song in praise of his wife, declaring her to be zaftig, and one for Woman herself, selected parts of Whom he will with great reverence name. Selah.

Blessed be the klezmer band and the musicians from Madrid's plaza de la corrida, united for this day, who will play what sounds like a cross between "Bei Mir Bist Du Schon," as interpreted by Sammy Cahn, and "Pasodoble," the toreadors' grand entrance march.

With gladness and rejoicing shall we jig, execute a veronica, or link arms and dance the hora around the Ark of the Covenant, here represented by a wedding cake in the shape of Yeats's tower at Ballylee.

As we do so, mark, ye Wasps, how we kick loose from our shoes sand from Tel Aviv, each grain the eye of history looking straight at you; industrial dust from the streets of Cork; and Andalusian clay, walked on by Lorca and still dreaming his dreams, like this wedding born of a Minnesota woman impregnated by a cosmic wind.

Therefore shall I take from my pocket, like a matador sliding a sword from its sheath, a handkerchief of one hundred per cent Irish linen and give it to the bride and groom to hold between their hands as they circle each other.

For the harp of Israel and the harp of the green isle shall be one.

As enthusiastically as townspeople carried Manolete in triumph through the squares of Cordoba and as easily as Buck Mulligan raised his bowl of lather in mockery of the sacred Host to begin the eternity of June 16, 1904, will eight banderilleros lift the bride and groom upon two chairs and sway them with tender mercies above the heads of the applauding congregation to the measures of "The Lass of Aughrim."

Let the glass goblet from which the bride and groom drink brim with Guinness, its lacy foam as pure as the dew that descended upon the mountains of Zion, and the groom stomp on the glass as the rabbi shouts, "Ole!" and "Slainte!"

Let the moment of truth upon this occasion be the taking of identical vows which, like sword blades flashing at five o'clock in the afternoon, doubly pierce the hearts of all fathers present.

And let Molly Bloom, even if she should arrive late and out of breath in a rush after concluding some necessary and herein tactfully unnamed business in Dublin, interpret, at least for her own purposes, the resounding "Amen" not as "So be it," which confirms the past, but as "Yes," which declares—as tables laden with steaming kosher corned beef and paella wait in the antechamber—an appetite for the future.

Jon Davis

THE BAIT

This is not an elegy because the world is full of elegies and I am tired of consoling and being consoled. Because consolation is unsatisfying and even tenderness can do nothing to stop this loss, this dying, this viciousness among men. And god just complicates, offering justice like the cracker I place in this mousetrap. Then the frantic mouse hands pushing against the metal bar, the kicking and bucking, the fall from the shelf, more kicking, one eye bulging, the lips lifted and the little yellowed teeth clamped on the small crumb of goodness that was not goodness but something alluring and, finally, dumb—without equivalent in the human world. Just food he couldn't have. *My* food and what that means in the scale of human affairs. I didn't want to listen to this mouse scrabbling among the graham crackers, chewing into the can of grease, leaving a trail of greasy, orange, rice-like shits in the cabinet under the sink. I didn't want to clean those up every morning; I didn't want to be awakened in the night. I set the trap; the trap smashed his skull; he kicked awhile and he died. I tossed him, trap and all, into the dunes. But I was saying something about god and justice. I was saying this is not an elegy and why. Because pain is the skin we wear? Because joy is that skin also? Because . . . look: I had a brother and he died. I didn't cause it; I couldn't stop it. He got on his motorcycle and rode away. A car turned in front of him and that began his dying. How terrible for everyone involved. Do I sound bitter? I felt the usual guilts: Did I love him enough? Did I show it? It happened eleven years ago and what I remember: Looking out at the lawn, September and a breeze; watching him ride—flash of red gas tank, brown leather jacket; the sound of the bike; what we said, which I recall as a kind of gesture, the sound of *what are you doing,* some dull rhythm and *see you later.* The phone call. The drive to the hospital. I think I drove but I can't be sure. We drove the wrong way down a one way street and I remember feeling responsible. I cried most of the time. I knew he was dying. My brother's girlfriend asked me *Why are you crying?* and I couldn't say or else I sobbed *It's bad I know it's bad.* Then we were taken into a green room and he was dead. I curled on a red plastic chair. My body disappeared or seemed to. I was looking for my brother; a nurse called me back: *Your family needs you.* I came back. But why am I telling you this? Because I want you to love me? To pity me? To understand I've suffered and that excuses my deficiencies? To see how loss is loss and no elegy no quiet talk late at night among loved ones who suddenly feel the inadequacy of their love and the expression of that love can take it away? Or give it back? Perhaps even loss is lost? My brother is gone and the world, you, me, are not better for it. There was no goodness in his death. And there is none in this poem, eleven years later and still confused. An attempt, one might say, to come to terms with his death as if there was somewhere to come to, as if there were terms. But there is nowhere to come to; there are no terms. Just this spewing of words, this gesture neither therapy nor catharsis nor hopelessness nor consolation. Not elegy but a small crumb. An offering.

Jon Davis

THE FROGS

Fourth of July and the children have grown miserable from turning and turning their wobbly cartwheels, from jumpkicking the forces of evil that throng about us, from dumping Kool-Aid on the younger children to attract our flagging attentions. These children who are capable of beauty and joy— "Look, Dad! A moth!"—but who quickly weary of the world's surprises as we weary, the parents of all this joy, who wear our silly striped ties—the badges of our race, the honors; who bang our heads against the daily task; who flop on our chaise longues and rattle the ice in our drinks; who bolt from our homes at midlife, then return to hammer back the boards through which we burst and live out our lives, pails under all the leaks. Who then fill the wagon with children and drive to a mountaintop to watch meteorites, stars dying across the sky so beautifully we rattle the ice in our drinks and remember the monastery we passed on the drive up, those poor monks who have no cluttered lives against which to measure such purity. And today we sneak four cars to the frog pond, 17th hole, Manchester Country Club, where we tie monofilament to fishing poles, squares of red flannel to monofilament, and dangle those squares before the frogs. They turn to face them, mistaking them for butterflies or moths. They leap and wrap their sticky tongues around the flannel, and we, shouting and whooping, fling them onto the fairway, where they flop and sprawl, where we chase them, where they extricate their tongues and hop, stunned, in whatever direction they face. Poor frogs. Poor frogs. Poor deluded creatures.

Jon Davis

IN HISTORY: I

Everyone knew him. Knew, but the radio swayed the room with a sweet jazz—saxophone monologue, then the whole quartet with something quick and to the point, then muted trumpet—so she couldn't hold his image. She heard her brother saying "Watch this!" Saw him and felt and heard him rolling down the sidewalk in '68 on a skateboard. How could she piece this together? And the sax saying, "How could you / How could you / How could you / How could you do what you done?" It was unmistakable. This time it was Bird muscled up and somehow barely sketching those notes. His whole life a mess and this sweet song. They all knew their neighbor. Knew how he moved beyond the blinds. Sometimes she saw his finger tugging the blinds the way her mother would pull down the corner of her eye to drip the medicine in. He was back there—sick, afraid—and they were shooting baskets or walking the children to the park. If you thought about it too much the world became intolerable. In this song the saxophone says, "We were down at Camarillo when the man came up to me and said / How could you do it / How could you do what you done?" They all circled the neighborhood while the bombs, no, *ordnance,* fell into Iraq. While the Scuds flared into the Jordanian night. While the World Bank engineered the end of life in the Amazon. *You could do this,* she thought. It was your duty: To stop at the Handi-Mart, the video store, the bakery. To wander the aisles of Penneys, your wallet fat with expectation. What if we all bought the right car or leaned our houses into the sun? If we ate fewer burgers or biked the eight miles to work? But he was watching them. And all she could see was the break in the blinds.

Jon Davis

IN HISTORY: II

The room was an emblem for loneliness—no toast in the toaster, blinds
carefully parted. One finger, tugging. The neighborhood was full of
strangers. He recognized that. They argued in front of, no, *behind* their
picture windows. The bullet would have already entered, piercing the
newly reupholstered davenport. No: *couch*. That was the name history
had found for it. "Late in the Twentieth Century there was a great
spiritual awakening." Announcers on some channels kept saying that.
It was a voice-over while the many well-groomed Americans looked
skyward. Later they would play the Super Bowl. Everyone had to watch
or be left speechless at break time. The man entered the woman from
behind. Later they would pass a law. He couldn't help feeling that ob-
jects were pressing up against his eyes. He tried to push them away. If
he could have painted what he saw. If he could have written it down.
The crowd was cheering in unison. In unison, they wanted the quarter-
back dead or maimed. Outside, a building rose until it filled the window.
There were no shots. Not yet. But he couldn't help feeling he had
caused them. He had wanted to move the couch. To hang the Monet on
the wall above the stereo. He had wanted to obliterate his feelings. Quit
his job. Burn the house. He had wanted to place a single rose in a thin,
crystal bud vase. He muted the television with the remote. The woman
moaned a little; he whimpered, grateful. Opening his eyes he saw the
building, people slapping hands: 49er fans. *Gold rush.* History was
incomprehensible. Intolerable. The blinds were barely parted. The bul-
let already tearing through fabric, the cotton batting splashing around
the bullet. An emblem of his sickness. He should kiss her afterward.
He should explain himself to the dust motes circulating in the afternoon
light. But she was gone. He was listening to the Pentagon spokesman:
"Bomb damage assessment is an art not a science." He wondered
about the implications of this confusion. And why did he think of it
now? We leave him there, wondering. We resist his attempts to draw
us into the puzzle. He leans to touch the already unscarred fabric.

Jon Davis

THE COMMON MAN

(In petto)

He was writing for the common man, but the common man was sleeping in his favorite chair, was dragging his bread through the yolk. He was writing for the common man, but Michael Jordan was peripateticating spectacularly through the crepuscular den. He was writing for the common man, but the six-pack, the film starring the former bodybuilder, the *ha ha* of pure evil having its face thrust into the gaping machinery, the unalloyed pleasure of the home team (good) versus the visitors (evil). He was writing for the common man, secretly nursing his contempt for the common man. Wanting to *improve* him. Wanting to make him see, to acknowledge, to embrace the murkiness of human motives. To make him squirm in his favorite chair. To make him awaken in the claws of a dream. To make him walk out into the morning of fog-webbed pastures, creaking milk trucks, children called into the open with their readers and lunch boxes, the horses wickering in their undersized corrals. He was writing for the common man, but the common man was balancing his coffee between his legs, was sitting between two masons in a red dump truck. Had his feet up on the tool bag, his knees leaned far right, anticipating the long throw into third. He was writing for the common man, secretly thinking *all is lost.* But the sun in the east, the moon still floating, the *larval* moon still floating in the western sky. The common man already out, walking his property line. Already out, waxing the Camaro with the common woman. Already out, stopping the BMW to pull prayer plumes from the road-killed bluebird—so delicate, wings half extended, toes locked on (perched on) nothingness, the eyes shut tight against the promise of light and time. Already out, leaping from the scaffold—like a spider rappelling from ceiling to floor—vines wrapped tight around his ankles, then the sudden jolt, cloud of dust, the upside-down writhing, the whoops and shouts, the welcome into manhood. Already out, being struck by the poetries of transformation—sunlight fluttering on the truck hood, shadows puddled under junipers and piñons, crows arcing in the cymophanous dawn.

Aleš Debeljak

In this moment, in the twilight of a cold room, thunder approaches from
a distance, through storm windows and dusty panes, in late afternoon,
the water in the pot doesn't boil, when fish gasp under the ice, when
half-asleep you tremble, as if without hope, when a pack—a herd of
shivering stags left the dried marshes deep in the woods and came to
the gardens in town, this fleeting instant, when the cold slices through
your spine, when hardened honey cracks in jars, when the thought of a
woman's hand—laid on the forehead of the dying—comes closer and
closer, when from the depths of memory destroyed villages you wanted
to forget begin to rise, when guilt and truth burn your stomach, when
frightened pheasants are flushed from tapestries hanging on the wall,
when guards leaving their posts whistle to one another, piercing the air,
when a sharp stone breaks your skull, should I remind you now that
your wounded body won't be any different than the shadow a solitary
bush casts across the trampled earth, east of Eden?

Translated from the Slovenian
by **Christopher Merrill**
(with the author)

Aleš Debeljak

Indifferently, he watched her through the shadows of furniture casually arranged in the narrow room, through a thin curtain drawn across the mirror hanging in the wardrobe, through a shaft of sunlight and dust splitting the room in half. She was fast asleep, head buried under the sheets where the pillow should have been, one shoulder bare, lost to the world. Her hands, her unpolished nails lay on the blanket pulled over her stomach, rising and falling with each breath. Stained sheets, previous guests, other lives. Or was it only his eyes blurring from gazing so long? The curve of her arm covering her dark nipple, the fallen strap of her nightgown. On her shoulder a band of light, as if through a veil, gently slipping over the down below her neck. Maybe he was a little tired. Not impatient. He thought: why here? So many other places, and yet here, always here?

New York City, September 1986

Translated from the Slovenian
by **Christopher Merrill**
(with the author)

Chard deNiord

THE MUSIC

If fish are notes in the river, then the song is never the same, even if the water is. Heraclitus was wrong. The current is motion is all. You touch a dancer as she pirouettes and she's still the same dancer. So there is a song that never gets played because the fish are always swimming in a way that rejects notation? If they stopped where they are right now, would they configure a song? Are they swimming, therefore, forever toward a melody? If so, you could say then that any song is the prescient catch of a school of fish at various depths, a quick and natural analogue for composition, the trout song, the bass song, the perch song. But the mind is the antinomy of a river, says Mr. Tsu. It is not the song beneath the surface that the fish suggest, for those songs never exist in time, but the fixed clear notes above the surface that are pinned to a sheet, on bars. The music we hear is played by musicians who have learned the difference between an idea and a score. So, Kepler was wrong also about the spheres, and Scriabin about the spectrum, and David about the hills. None of these things contain music. Only the mind thinks they do. Only the mind would ruin their silence with a symphony.

Peter Desy

DAD'S HOME

My dead father woke up living in the bedroom next to mine. Nothing had changed in twenty years; I had never grieved for him, so when he came down to breakfast we said hello in a perfunctory way and he fried two eggs before going to work. He said it was nothing like you'd expect on the other side, no Jesus or anything like that, so he came home here, to the house on Indiana Street, back to his desk job, back to be 'nothing but a goddam paycheck' for his family again, who, I told him, had all left, and his wife had died and I stayed on to be an alcoholic like him. He said to watch my mouth and I told him I was a college professor for ten years now, a publisher of articles, an instructor of youth. So what's new? I asked.

It's an exponential growth industry without a market, galaxies of crap and trash there, oppressive, like the Henry Ford Museum. A near-infinitude of cars, chariots, carts, socks, bones, capes, unguent jars— goods substantial and insubstantial, things strange and things familiar.

It's annoying, though. You *know* everything, and so fast that at first it's kind of transcendent, but you soon reduce it all to a few principles, like a three-note musical scale. So much for intelligibility and the empirical spirit you subscribe to.

Well, the flavors you taste, a thousand simultaneously if you like. Your tongue tip's a million buds. All that. But then there are the vast abstractions, just like Plato said. No one can put it all together, though—all that multiplicity! The juicy 'world' and the sculpturesque beauty of the Forms. Too much tension for my inelastic nature. So much for your 'little-islands-of-order-in-the-sea-of-chaos' kind of thinking.

The farther you go in, the more light plays tricks on you. You think you're heading toward the source, but there's a confusion of brightness everywhere. And everything's on the verge of ecstasy, but whatever moves doesn't get completed. It made me want to do something ugly, like paint a rainbow with a broom. So here I am, not ready to take any more questions. I think I'll have tuna for lunch, no salt, and just a little water.

Ray DiPalma

DILATION

Visibly awake meant an entire geography, bounded by invention and a mountain. An introspection lifted out of an education. The hexagonal chamber made for the octagonal room in the circular tower. You think: the assertions require marketable categories. Compunctions and trivial investigations. The moon shaped like a page in a book. August, Thursday, where is the sun? It must be morning by now. In a corner of the room a series of brass rings, beyond the table and chair, beyond the pile of papers and dropped books. Dilated information scored among the subtly inaudible. [I can barely hear you, but I'd like you to have all my money.] The yield: NUMERICAL VENTRILOQUY. A contraction of resources appropriate to the situation—strictly on a need-to-know basis. Illustrations of an inexpensive sort, admittedly, but as dignified as possible. Numbers and letters that calculate the lower edge of a black cloud. Partway there you can always go out and buy yourself some money. Avoid banks, publishing, and the art market. Calculations properly maintained provide more than the gist of a sensible arrangement. The interpolation of something perfectly legible. The burnt pages retaining certain details of what had been misunderstood. Their impassive faces lifted upwards, a small group of people stand in a far corner of the room waiting to use the telephone. Islands that deserve more than an entire wall. The years pass while the numbered days remain as thickly dispersed as any euphemism. Sotto visu, but fanatical. Recrimination and scorn pulled out of the shadows only to return as geometry. Smart dark scraps of the ACCUNUMEROID. This is what he found, this is what he lives off, and this is what he has.

Liljana Dirjan

THE URBAN LIFE

These mornings, when I pass alongside Parisian fish vendors, I witness blank, white, frozen men in the process of wage and capital, spreading out fish fresh from the sea and just off the boat. The unraveled forms sparkle in the sheen of coin and mother-of-pearl, luminous shocks of ice pounded down in stalls, the clear light of January. I suffer their separate deaths, their stared-through eyes, their void. Such jettisoned and mute nakedness . . . so suddenly I need to feel my heart beneath my coat to convince me who I am—my clean presence; my still warm, still life.

Translated from the Macedonian
by **P.H. Liotta**

Stuart Dybek

ALPHABET SOUP

In this place the soup was what one came for—alphabet soup for the Language poets—and a clear broth for everyone else. Here, ordering a steaming bowl of soup could be like visiting an oracle. Soup was a kind of lens: "a monocle for the mouth," in the unforgettable phrase of the renowned poet-dentist, Victor Guzman, DDS.

Despite its storefront appearance, it wasn't just another ethnic restaurant. It was too cosmopolitan for that. American poets of the International school table-hopped, suavely reciting their poems in what sounded like English translations. In those days, the so-called One-of-the-Boys-Gang of surrealists ate there, too. Do you remember them?

Adjacent to the restrooms, an old phone booth to which plywood siding had been hammered and a cross affixed, served as a makeshift confessional where the unrepentant Confessional poets lined up to dine, kneeling before their soup as if it could forgive them.

A table in a corner, way in the back, with only a single chair was where the Hermetics ate—one at a time.

The Academics frequented another place, just across the street, Bloom's Deli, where, to their clamorous orders, the bored Mrs. Bloom said nothing beyond *yes yes yes,* punctuated by an occasional *oy vey* as her customers deconstructed the brisket.

Ah! these allusions of grandeur!

At all the little tables, hunched over simmering controversies, various groups of poets slurped their soup. They had gathered like opposing, neighborhood softball teams gather at a neutral corner tavern after their games on Friday night in order to recount their exploits, to total and retotal the score, to study the rankings and their own particular statistics, to ascribe errors, dissect reputations, erect legends. Instead of Bud's Bombers or the Popes of Pilsen Park, they had names like the Formalist Strokers, the Regionalist Whackers, the Multicultural Pounders, and the Dukes of Deep Image. The greasy light of soup illuminated their faces and made their eyes gleam. There were the Beats, sipping soup from a burbling hookah, the Political Poets memorializing the exploited between brimming mouthfuls, and the One-of-the-Girls-Gang of women poets, their spoons all clacking until invariably from some table or other someone would cry, "Garçon! there's a fly in my soup!"

A rare silence would befall the room, all eyes watching as the Garçon comes rushing to the table.

"There's a fly in my soup!"

"I see," the Garçon says. "Allow me," and he reaches into the bowl, unzips the soup's fly, and a penis, limp as a noodle, floats out.

"I say, what sort of soup have you served me? Take it away, take it to that empty window table reserved for the audience."

Russell Edson

SLEEP

There was a man who didn't know how to sleep; nodding off every night into a drab, unprofessional sleep. Sleep that he'd grown so tired of sleeping.

He tried reading The Manual of Sleep, but it just put him to sleep. That same old sleep that he had grown so tired of sleeping . . .

He needed a sleeping master, who with a whip and a chair would discipline the night, and make him jump through hoops of gasolined fire. Someone who could make a tiger sit on a tiny pedestal and yawn . . .

Russell Edson

BREAD

I like good looking bread. Bread that's willing. The kind of bread that's found in dreams of hunger.

And so it was that I met such a bread. I had knocked on a door (I sometimes do that to keep my knuckles in shape), and a women of huge doughy proportions (she had that unbaked, unkneaded look) appeared holding a rather good-looking loaf of bread.

I took a bite and the loaf began to cry . . .

Russell Edson

THE TRAVELING CIRCUS

A white-faced clown lying in the gutter like an old tennis shoe. The circus has left town . . .

The last time the circus left town, it left the fat lady dumped on the sidewalk like a pile of cottage cheese wearing lingerie.

Packing and unpacking, the circus always on the move, always forgetting something. One time even forgetting to leave town . . .

Russell Edson

BALLS

Two roly-poly men are pretending to be bowling balls.

Get off my property, says someone on whose property the roly-poly men are pretending to be bowling balls.

We're too big to be golf balls.

Get off my property, you goof balls.

We were thinking about cannon balls, but bowling balls are more social.

Social?

Oh yes, we're social types.

But you're too roly-poly for social lives.

That's why we thought to debut the social world as bowling balls. We're really rather good. We even have the holes . . .

Russell Edson

THE PORTRAIT

Someone with a mirror advertises himself as a portrait painter.
Could you do me in oil?

Boil you in oil? Vegetable, of course, healthier than animal fat. Or
would you prefer flyspecks on a cracker to go with that thing around
your neck? Incidentally, what is that thing, a hangman's noose?

Oh that, that's my collar and leash, my handler waits for me in
heaven.

It looks more like a bandage. Was your head part of the French
Revolution, and then sewn back?

No no, an umbilical cord which my mother helped me tie into a nice
knot.

In the last moments of this particular writing, the portrait, which has
taken years to complete, is finally finished with the speed of light . . .

Russell Edson

THE ANTIQUE SHOP

There was a man who wanted to buy an old man in an antique shop, how much for that old man?

You do me too much honor, but owing to my youth I'm not for sale, smiled the old man who was standing behind a counter of antique bellybuttons.

How much for that piece of biological trash?

One man's trash is sometimes another man's treasure, smiled the old man, who was now wearing a bellybutton on his forehead like a third eye.

You're old enough to be dead, said the man, but still young enough to be put on a pole for a scarecrow. So how much for the nasty old man?

He's not ripe enough to be sold as an authentic antique, smiled the old man who was now wearing the bellybutton on one of his earlobes.

By the way, what's with that bellybutton?

Oh that, I'm trying to find the right place to grow my new umbilical cord.

But you're too old for an umbilical cord.

I know, smiled the old man, isn't it wonderful? . . .

Nikos Engonopoulos

MARIA OF THE NIGHT

On the day immediately following my death—or should I say my execution—I picked up all the newspapers to find out everything I could concerning the particulars. It seems I was led out onto the scaffold under heavy guard. I was purportedly wearing a yellow overcoat, a woven necktie, and a helmet. My hair resembled bristles—the bristles of a paintbrush perhaps, or perhaps the brush used in the application of tar. Afterwards they dumped my body in a remote swamp, which the Frenchman Descartes had once used as a hideout, and where for years now the corpse of glorious Karamanlakis has lain, prey to vultures and to a temple-slave by the name of Euterpe. And while there were rumors regarding my wherabouts at the time—some said Maracaibo in South America, others claimed Pasolimani in Pireas—the plain truth is that I was in Elbasan (Albania). And the only thing of note I read at the time was a long-winded letter from my dear and only friend, the Italian Guilliamo Tsitzes, whom I have never met and whom, moreover, I suspect has never existed. In a word, the entire contents of the letter consisted in the following: "You"—meaning, of course, Polyxena—"You are an old gramophone with a bronze horn, sailing under a black sail."

Translated from the Greek
by **Martin McKinsey**

Elke Erb

RIP VAN WINKLE

Five peeled tree trunks I saw as I came to: my bed, and puddles and scattered tins. I recognized our trenches by the concave yellow clay walls, but found not a single soldier. Ergo, war must have gone home, the comrades didn't want to disturb my sleep, didn't wake me.

I hoisted myself to the edge of the trench and scanned woods and fields: May, blinding sun. In the woods, that nevertheless shrank back in fear, a cuckoo calling. Here I was, alone, a senile machine gun, a toothless cur that couldn't fasten on any-body, in woods that nevertheless shrank back in fear.

Translated from the German
by **Rosmarie Waldrop**

Clayton Eshleman

CONSTRICTOR

The old boy's club of the bad in cog with the old boy's club of the good, thugs intent upon natal revenge create their shadow brothers, cops intent upon secondary revenge, in whose basement is the same natal plight, these two knots of men coiling through history, the Mafia and the police, the vampire and the clergyman, the Flynt and Falwell Inc., constrictors around the bodies of women, their women, of children, their children, the detective sits up in bed, it's his monthly period, gush of nightmare, constrictor of male bonding, binding, male moulting, Sepik Delta painted men jacking off in a tight circle, no escape for the malefic fly that if not let out will rot into the men its egg power, its maggot beauty, to be reborn as sacred killer, sacred defender, constrictor of the womanless male knot, the need to turn the victim into sacred property, the toes of the lynched offered for sale, roasted liver of a black boy, trophy streaming with the dead peacock eyes now of amazonal foliage, knot worked as a cud, buddy love in which killing replaces buggery, thwarted male Eros, Germanic morning of armies like fire ants moving through the edible forest of cities, the man who would saw his face off before he would kiss another man, the woman who arrived at the back alley abortion room with eight feet of her intestines in a paper sack.

Gary Fincke

THE HISTORY OF PASSION WILL TUMBLE THIS WEEK

Because the state is slicing off the dangerous scales of the cliff over one of its highways, the newspaper suggests a reunion, asks former defacers to gather, and I park north of Pittsburgh, among dozens of cars, nearly a hundred of us quoting the graffiti of desire. Doreen and Clarice, Monica and Donna—I try to read the nearby faces like name tags at a conference, guess whether or not they're still paired with Chuck and Ron, Woody and Buck. And in this hand-over-hand history of lust, I think Gary sounds so formal that I'm the fool who was never in love, that Gary + Sharon, still visible, is a forgery because only the Butch I once was would have risked himself seventy feet above this traffic, that nobody else at the base of this blackboard would have struggled into danger and printed anything but his nickname before he added the full spelling of the girl he'd stay with forever.

Lawrence Fixel

A LITTLE KITCHEN MUSIC

. . . . Krista in the kitchen. She studies the assembled ingredients—the carrot, the purple onion, the celery. A painter of still lifes, her attention rests there: the colors, textures, the way they are arranged speak to her. She shakes off the momentary reverie: let's get this done, back to work . . . One of the guests wanders in, offers to help. They talk about this and that. She tells the friend, a woman of her own age, that she could use some help—but later. Another comes in, asks for a glass of water. She points to where the glasses are stored, and to the bottled water in the pantry . . .

*

. . . . It is going well. A long time since she has prepared dinner just for friends. A matter of timing. She moves back and forth, eyes the clock on the wall, the pots and pans on the stove. Someone has put on a record; the music reaches her through the fragrances, the sounds, the noise of voices from the other rooms. She recognizes something of what she hears in the music: *A Haydn Quartet? Can't be sure. Perhaps one of the lesser known . . .*

*

. . . . The windows are beginning to steam up. She turns on the oven fan. The noise takes over. The music disappears. The windows remain smudged. She opens the back door to the pantry. There's enough breeze to make the gas jets flutter. She hesitates, decides to leave the door open. Last time she was frying something in the black iron skillet, and the smoke set off the fire alarm . . . It doesn't take much to set it off. I'm doing what I can, as best I can. All this activity for a painter of still lifes. That's what I am now—just that, nothing more. Mother, lover, that is still there—but not like before. Remember: it's your own life, whatever that is, whoever is here, for as long as they stay: *the necessary company.*

*

. . . . She will know when it is done. Hopefully it all comes out together. They will soon be sitting at the same table. Looking into each other's faces. Listening to each other's voices. As real as they—or rather *we*—can be. It's not a story, not a movie: we can't be sure how anything, this meal included, will turn out. Still I am trying to put this taste in these dishes—the taste that love invites, that friendship furthers. A little sustenance, a little ceremony, and something that makes it seem like an occasion. Did I read that somewhere? *Haydn, my dear, sorry you couldn't make it. Better luck next time.*

Lawrence Fixel

THE SMILE AT THE FOOT OF THE LADDER

> If there's one among you, or among you one,
> who climbed the ladder of his own identity,
> he shook the hand of Mister Agony. . . .
>
> —A.T. Rosen

1.

 . . . . The painful ascent: hands gripping the sides, step after step, not knowing how much further we can go. As if it were indeed some risky venture, on a sheer rock face, that we have foolishly undertaken— perhaps to prove something, or answer someone else's challenge. . . . But this is just one reading of the poet's words. Better perhaps to set aside the warning, the cautionary note, the metaphor itself, and return to the literal, familiar object. Precisely what you can see for yourself: stored in the garage, or propped against a wall that needs cleaning or painting. . . .

2.

 . . . . Have we moved too quickly here, or in the wrong direction? Perhaps even more than either image or metaphor, our real need is for a concept that the ladder itself involves both the horizontal and the vertical. Something designed a long time ago by someone with a direct, useful task to perform. One that involves both ascending and descending. . . .

3.

 . . . . But of course we have left out something. We have forgotten that we still have a story to tell. One that we have heard, read, or invented, imagined. . . . Ladder in a romantic novel. He finds one conveniently placed beside the house. And there he goes: in moonlight, or hidden among the dark shadows, up, up, toward the arms of his beloved. . . . Or more seriously, in desperate circumstance, the last chance for escape of the men trapped in the mine. . . .

4.

     . . . . And where out of all this comes the notion of standing at the foot of the ladder, with no inclination, no desire, to ascend? Even if it is only that "one among you" for whom it is enough to feel the earth under his feet. . . . True he has missed the heights, the excitement of the ascent, the panoramic view of peaks and valleys. . . . He feels ready to move on; for he has witnessed enough to let him know he has found his rightful place. This must be one of those moments, he tells himself, when one can simply walk past, praising the small beauties of the small world. . . .

Charles Fort

T. S. ELIOT WAS A NEGRO

During Eliot's senior year in college after he lost a copy of The Pardoner and wept he listened closely to Edison's faint recording of Whitman's voice at the Library of Congress and the words and the coals inside the Victrola curled the lime on his top hat and the nimble conversation put Eliot at ease and each image echoed inside his rather large ears and he brought them closer to the flip side of the red vinyl with only one pale slip of the poet's tongue and he learned on the evening tide of his mulatto life how the smoke signals from his pipe circled the town green of his hometown and the hourglass inside his father's vest pocket gave a warning to the citizens of the world and as their children marched behind the blue tail of the wonder mule and sang in celebration the doctor looking out over the parade finally realized what had made a young Eliot dream about the city workers who tossed Eliot's plague caked body into death's carriage left stalled by the helmsman on the corner of Bishop and State in New Haven who stood before the temple under a prehistoric shadow and years later recorded how Eliot had read poems and lectured to his students from this same corner in a wedding of laughter and science until he awakened in sweat as the constable held Eliot's skull clean as a monkey's jaw above the altarstone two and a half miles from Yale University and thirty-six miles from the rose garden at Elizabeth Park in Hartford and while on his knees before his God he remembered exactly how he had fallen asleep in the afternoon in his mother's arms after he had breastfed and listened to her whisper the nursery rhyme of the wonder mule who stood like a mantis on its burnt hind hooves and fell dead on its raw side as the town clock burned and collapsed in snow and the citizens with twins their muse and human militia perished in flames the day he was born.

Richard Garcia

CHICKENHEAD

Chickenhead makes me think of Jesus. Even though Jesus died on the cross for our sins and Chickenhead was just a hood who died hanging from a meat hook. First, take the Romans—Italian, right? In other words, gangsters. Take hanging from a cross and hanging from a meat hook. Both ways, you die slow.

Chickenhead used to shoot the heads off chickens in his backyard when he was a kid. Jesus used to play with birds when he was a kid too. Except, instead of blowing them apart he would put them together.

Chickenhead was a big shot on the block. In more ways than one, since he weighed three hundred pounds. When Chickenhead got in the back of his Cadillac it would tilt to one side. Jesus was big in his neighborhood too. But he was skinny. When Jesus would get on a donkey— maybe it was an old, decrepit, almost dead donkey—that donkey would trot along skimming over stones as if it had wings.

Jesus made people mad. Chickenhead made people mad. Skimming a little off the top is O.K., it's expected. But after Chickenhead bought that second Cadillac and after what he did to that Gypsy girl in the back room of the cleaners with her dad forced to watch, he had to go.

The Romans had dice. We had dice. The Romans had a wooden cross. We had a meat hook. The Romans had spears and vinegar. We had a bucket of cold water and one of those electric cattle pokers.

Chickenhead hung there. We'd give him a splash and an electric goose once in a while. His whole body would shimmer, all blubbery. Took Jesus three hours. Took Chickenhead three days.

Jesus got famous. First guy to beat Death at his own game. Nobody remembers Chickenhead but me. And if some stranger, a cop maybe, asked, Did I know Chickenhead? I'd play it safe just like Saint Peter when he heard that cock crow, once, twice, three times, and I'd say, I never knew nobody named Chickenhead.

Val Gerstle

MOM TOLD ME TO GROW UP AND WIN THE NOBEL PRIZE

Mom told me to grow up and win the Nobel Prize. She taught me how
to check my breasts for cancer and made sure I knew who Cezanne
was. When I was sixteen, I put on cologne that smelled like chrysan-
themums and let a pornographer take pictures of me sitting in icy water
that made my nipples stick out like chimneys. On weekends he took me
to the Parkette Drive-In. I saw "Kill and Be Killed" six times. The year
I turned eighteen I got an apartment with a carpet, and took to wearing
kneesocks and stickpins. A football player who became an insurance
salesman after he tore the ligaments in his knee married me late that
summer. The wedding was small, but I got a hotpad set, pink toilet
cover, yogurt maker and fly-zapper. My parents sent us to Sarasota for
the honeymoon. A year later I was bored with diapers and daytime TV,
so I took a plane to California and changed my name and hair color. I
met a wiry young women who was doing research work with carrier
pigeons. Since she was middle-class and I suddenly wasn't, she took
me to lunch at a place with dark air and leather seats and stone jugs.
We drank beer and she gave me a key to her apartment so I could have
someplace decent to eat sandwiches and take showers and sleep. Then
I went uptown and got a job as a typist in an ad agency. The Director
liked me because I was young and didn't talk and typed fast. I was
happy bringing home a paycheck each weekend. I made just enough to
buy soap and sandwiches and a couple more tulip print dresses, and
occasionally a luxury, like a bracelet for the scientist on her birthday.
We put on our pajamas and sat in front of the TV and celebrated with
crab-meat soup and gin straight from the bottle.

Amy Gerstler

MYSTERIOUS TEARS

A homicide detective has the grave responsibility of resolving the most serious criminal act one human can commit against another. Therefore, we bear an important burden when called upon to investigate a death, for we stand in the dead person's shoes, so to speak, to protect his or her interests against everybody else's.

We're lucky she was killed in snow. This kind of old, crumbly snow's impressionable. Her January garden. Pathetic. Shows she had a soft spot for lost causes: winter gardening at this elevation, and that Dutchman. He's handsome. I'll give him that. He'll be Miss Popularity in prison. Deer footprints all over. Plants nibbled to nubs—a real deer cafeteria. Remember that case with an African parrot as sole witness? "Don't, please don't!" is all it kept screaming. Talking birds freak me out. I wouldn't let my partner leave me alone with it. I'd be more comfortable hearing a beer can or matchbook speak. Snapped-off prairie grass: sure sign of a fight.

The Dutchman lies on his back in a holding cell, complaining to the ceiling "I'm starved! When do we eat?", eyes hot with mysterious tears. He's got such a mob yelling in his head, voices from various centuries—Calamity Jane, Job, one of Hitler's assistants, that little boy from the "Lassie" TV show—he probably can't remember which one convinced him to kill her. Maybe they ganged up on him.

Till each crime's solved I carry a post-mortem Polaroid of the victim's face in my wallet—which has gotten a lot fatter than I'd like. Pictures of my kids I keep in a different compartment back here, with the cash.

Nestled in the crotch of this dwarf tree: an unexpected find. A nest and five bluish eggs scrawled with tiny purple hieroglyphics. My wife, one of the happy fraternity of naturalists, would know how to read these. I'm stumped. Slate-colored junco or common nighthawk? Perhaps an olive-backed thrush. More witnesses who won't talk. That includes you, too, bloodstained leather gardening gloves, iron gate, dead vines, and worms curling and uncurling where we dug them up, like infants' fingers.

If the photographer's all through, let the dogs loose inside the hedge border awhile. Maybe they can sniff out some underpinnings and not just piss all over the crime scene, like last time.

My wife says no dwelling has more integrity than a well-made nest.

Our search should begin in the area immediately surrounding the body and proceed outward.

Apparently all he's done since his arrest is cry. Did the beefy Dutchman weep as he stabbed her, watched by primitive winter roses?

The badly scratched victim still brandishes a fork. Bits of heavily peppered egg cling to the tines. I think I saw a wound on the back of the Dutchman's hand that looked like a forkstab: four tiny holes. Let's check. Looks like she tried to defend herself with a trowel, too. She should have smashed him on the skull with the shovel. It was right there, at arm's reach.

I don't think mammals should die with their eyes open, do you? Blood gets fanned out around the neck kind of cape-like due to arterial gushing. Don't step in it! Little tangles of dark hair, just what might be caught in her comb some morning, skitter between the tree roots like shy spiders. Bet you twenty bucks some of her hair ends up lining a bird's nest next spring.

Gary Gildner

THE WOLVERINE

Word got around town: a wolverine was being shown in Rae Brothers parking lot. Some last-minute Christmas shoppers went to look. Many of the younger people had never seen one before, not up close like this. It lay curled in the back of a pickup, on the tailgate, and someone—a small girl—said it looked like a big fuzzy caterpillar. The man holding her hand said, "See those teeth? You wouldn't want to fool with them!" And somebody else asked, "What is it?" The ranger, who had received it from the trapper, said it was a male. About thirty pounds. He said he was surprised: wolverines were supposed to have been long gone from the area. The trapper was surprised too: he'd been after bobcat. He had his foot up on a rear tire and was leaning against his knee; his hat was pushed back; he could look down and see the animal as he talked. The man holding the small girl's hand asked what he used to catch it. "A snare," the other said. "With that good aircraft cable that don't kink." He shook his head at the surprise of it all, or at the snare's effectiveness, or maybe only as a kind of punctuation; and a couple of older men, whose eyes were watery-bright from age, shook their heads too. It got cold standing there in Rae Brothers parking lot, and people began drifting away. One of these, a girl, said to her boyfriend, "I hate those things." He laughed, then flung his arm around her neck, pulling her closer.

James Vladimir Gill

WORDS FOUND ABOVE A SWINGING GATE

Rest, head.

From a pillow recomposed fall crumpled bits of jaundiced note paper, stunned, enigmatic whispers left here, again, on a late Sunday afternoon. When? How do you write them? From what shadow of the mind do they come sauntering out, firefly prophecies?

Could they be dead flies swatted an eternity ago on the walls of constancy? See how they hang on now, precarious, encrusted wings entwined in a vine, refusing to let go.

Have you noticed how they watch us move into this Indian summer of ours, rupturing time and bone? Life to life, you once said, is a long walk in Toledo by failing light. Light enough that one can no longer hide.

Shouldn't we then, very quietly, and please, without another kindly nod, fold ourselves to rest and be endowed with special life, like those dolls blind people make?

Ray Gonzalez

BUSY

I am busy living in the new millennium. It fits well with the depression I left back in the twentieth century. I am happier now because I am older and fewer birds fly after me. If I could grow a beard, I would. If I could take my time in deciding what I think of my country, it would be easier to live here without thinking I have to have an opinion, cast a vote, or drink distilled water. I am not sure where I am going with this, but it is a fine season for confessing how we made it past the zero hour. Even the tiny spider crossing the white rug in the living room is going to make it into the first decade of the new awareness. I don't step on it or call my cat's attention to it. The little spider passes the leg of the sofa and disappears. I read in the newspaper about the 20,000 fish that were found dead in the Guadalupe River near San Antonio. It turns out it was fire ant mating season. After male fire ants mate with the females in mid-air, they die. When wildlife people cut open the dead fish to see what killed them, they found thousands of fire ants in their bellies. The toxic poison of the male fire ants killed the fish after they gorged on the falling insects. I am busy thinking about this because I used to live in the area and was attacked by fire ants several times. This thought fits with what I was going to say. I have two large windows in my office and a large desk. When I open any book in my office, I always use both hands.

Miriam Goodman

SHOPPING TRIP

I try on clothes with you and fifty other women in a mirrored room.
Down to my pantyhose and bra, I step into a dress and hold my breath.
The moment I know my body fails to fit, an apparition of my mother
comes and warns me not to get involved with you. You're fat and sad,
my mother says, wearing her half-size navy crepe, a window of lace at
her breast. She also shopped for bargains.

I'm seeking our reflection in the mirrors, heavy, unsexual, trying a
skin for the world. You look for slacks they can't see through. I look for
skirts that hide me, yet push forward to be noticed. The stockgirls in the
center of the room rehang the garments we discard like piles of novels
taken back to shelve. I don't know how to dress the role you'd have me
play: a woman who loves sex with women. It seems to me that I look
bad in everything.

I ask if your grown daughters love you. "They'd better," you say,
"since I don't love myself." We are alike in this as in less hidden things
and yet we look for love to make us new. So let's get out of here and go
pick up a turkey. We could slide our hands inside the carcass, roll them
in the slippery juices, thinking of each other, of delight. "Look, there's
the moon," I could tell you. And I could write you from the future:
"Remember when?" I have nostalgia for this chance, and for my mother.
And though I can't make love to you, I could make a turkey with her
watching.

David Greenslade

SPEAK UP

When a man does the shopping he makes a few mistakes. First, he buys a thousand stalks of broccoli. It was fresh, reduced and he wished he had a family to feed. Choosing bread, he pours wine across the blades of his plough. But there are bandits in the wheat and he left his rifle in the car. Buying a few slices of ham he is amazed at the purposeful faces of the women. They know where every penny goes, they also know a hoarder when they see one. He checks his trolley. Potatoes, newspaper, shoelaces, tobacco, beer and cake. Next time he'll make a list. He puts a little of the sugar back. He can't get used to it. He can hear his mother's voice advising him. She's dead so he tells her to speak up. She's giving him some bad advice. He's talking to a jar of jam. Is anybody *else* in there? Speak up!

Richard Gwyn

LIFTING THE VIRGIN

Her job is to keep the church clean, arrange the flowers, change the candles. At midday she cooks a meal for the priest. But her main concern is the well-being of the alabaster statues, especially the virgin. Last week, she tells me, they had to lift the statue of the virgin, move her awhile. "You can't imagine how much she weighed," she smiles, as though discussing a defiant but beloved child. The wind has stopped. Everything is quiet. I walk with the priest to the village bar. Afterwards, in the square, the children gather round, playing and chatting, as though they had known me all their lives. I am a stranger, who has walked into this tiny place and soon will wander on. The woman in the church, the priest, the sky, the children, the little square with its tree and two swings. A conspiracy of nouns. But the effect is of a flow between one thing and the next, on a journey that has lost all points of reference and offers only the salvation of continuity. Lifting this life-size model of the virgin provides a challenge to all that is unchanging in a village on a plain. She was so heavy. You can't imagine.

Leo Haber

THE GRINDER BARUCH ESPINOSA

The lenses he ground refracted another world, not the musky woods far beyond Amsterdam that surreptitiously opened into gently rolling plains of bare brown earth, muddy black in some places, dry and burnt umber in others; not the heavy gray haze of fetid air that sat on the landscape and made mystery of bogs and grainy trees on the canvas of the Dutch painters; not canals whose brackish waters twisted past silvery bridges and sly alleyways and gaudy gabled houses that would some day sequester Anne Frank until her forced liberation into the woeful world outside; not the bearded stooped elders of Rembrandt's vision with their own eyes socketed in sorrow and even a little fear as they proclaimed the law of the outcast against his way of seeing; but a world that transcended earth, air, water, fire—even people—and posited a God that would not be moved from stasis to concern Himself with any human thing, much less the grief of a mere stripling of twenty-six repudiated by his people.

Moses said to God, destroy me but do not harm your nation; Spinoza might have said the same had he thought that God was listening.

Still he prospers in our minds like Moses who alone saw the nape of God's neck and the holy knot of the dark phylactery; without Rembrandt's skills, Spinoza missed the finer faces, but with his ground lenses and his lisping soul he peered, in a stupor of joy, beyond the red blood of men and the golden glow of women and the shifting kaleidoscope of the shaded world into the colorless black hole eternal of God.

S. C. Hahn

OMAHA

Dawn leaves a highway of blood running down the bluffs into the Missouri.

At the Union Pacific roundhouse, the doors roll open with a screech of metal, and great engines haul the heat of August out into the day.

A block away from St. Frances Cabrini church in Little Italy, the face of Christ grows on a Big Boy tomato in Mrs. Antonia Cabriatti's garden. She sits at her kitchen window, drinking coffee with cream and eating anisette toast, wondering whether to cook the tomato or report it to Father Vitelli. She would like to eat the face of Christ as a sauce on a nice fritatta, but she could never confess that to the priest.

Down Tenth Street at the Praha Bakery, Jim Kovar puts another ball of rye dough on his baker's paddle and places it into the brick oven. It is the same motion his grandfather used when he was an artilleryman in the army of Emperor Franz Josef. Whenever people eat Kovar's rye bread they bite into caraway seeds, and that little shell bursts into a cloud of remembering: the bread at the older Preshyl girl's wedding feast, the roast duck with skin goose-pimpled as boys skinny-dipping in an early May stream, steam rising from potato dumplings and kraut, tart Pilsener beer, the prune and apricot kolachy. Ah, memory is a fat mid-wife, they say, and the future is a thin bride.

Over on Thirteenth Street, Maria Kutzowski sells a Tootsie Roll to the Cantu kid, whose father Hector works in one of the packing plants. She remembers when this whole neighborhood was Polish and Lithuanian, but her children have all moved to the west side. At least these Mexicans are good Catholics, she thinks, not like all the apostate Lutheran Danes up around north 30th Street. She went up there once, she says in Polish to her friends over beers at the Vistula Tavern, and felt like she was in a foreign country. Not a kerchief to be seen on the heads of the women! But she would like to go again, because the men are handsome . . .

It is like that all over the rest of Omaha this morning: in the black community north of Dodge Street, where people are having breakfast and thinking about what they will do after work this evening; in the old Jewish neighborhood over by Central High; in the Serbian blocks by the foundry; in the dwellings of the Swedes and the Germans and the Irish and the Greeks, all the way west to Boys Town.

In every house, in every heart is a packing plant built of the slow-fired bricks of experience, where dreams hang on steel hooks in cold storage.

Cecil Helman

THAT UFO THAT PICKED ON US

That UFO that came down that day. The one that picked on us, just us. Circular and silver, that almost whitening-grey and glistening one. Why us? The one that set fire to the cowshed, and did those mathematical things to the chickens, God rest their little souls. But why to us? Why then? Do you remember it, that so-called UFO? The one that divided Uncle Basil, and subtracted Aunty May? That silvery thing, silver-blue as a circular whale that swam, just like that, through the air. At great speed, just like this, look, just like that. But why us? Remember that UFO, remember that high electrostatic whine, and the aurora borealis that fell across the farm. The shadows in the fields. The old crops whitening. The shriek of radio, and all that fearful television. The pylons that ran in panic across the yard, trailing their wires behind them. The tractors that fought each other to death, inside the incubators. All those llamas then, and the wild rabbits, and the melted generator. All dead and gone, all of them, now. Even the fax machines, dead in their corral, among the crispy remains of Xerox and thyme. Do you remember that alleged UFO that landed among us that day? The one that took me so far away, and never brought all of me back again?

Bob Heman

GEOGRAPHY

There was a circle where the tower was built. There were three circles where the wife changed into salt. There was a square where the tablets were broken. A line was all that was left after the boat sailed by. The triangles indicated the place where the murders took place. The single dot represented the eye of the serpent. The mountain where the sacrifice didn't occur was the only horizon they were allowed.

Bob Heman

THIS TIME

This time the hand is made of clouds. The sky is a huge animal whose breathing has stopped. The climbers when they arrive are composed of different colors. One of them has forgotten to attach his lifeline. He is the only one who does not fall. He is constructed from a system made of hesitations. Each time he tries to speak, a different pause emerges to smother his incentive. The hesitations are named after the settlements the river never returned.

Brian Henry

THE INVITATION

"Casual" brings me here, my face a digital clock blinking from the power outage that left the Christmas turkey cold. The wind snaps limbs, fells a tree or two—no great downpour, just a drizzle, not worth the energy of wipers on passing cars. Interesting, that swirl of leaves, dead but refusing to be still. To bury a loved one one needs a good shovel, strong arms, and a good heart. A shame about that shih tzu being torn from its owner beside the money machine. Usually it's children, but I guess dogs make better gifts—easier to care for. This soirée, this festive affair, may place my life in order. The invitation was waiting for me, just for me, in that shopping cart. And I aim to please, once I find the house on this endless road.

Jennifer L. Holley

THE RUBBING

We both wake up in the night. On her way from the bathroom, she meets me in the kitchen, a glass of water in my hand. *Will you please rub my legs?* she asks. I take her arm, walk her back to bed. She stretches on top of the blanket, turns on her stomach, pulls off her turban, and spreads her fingers through the gray fuzz on her scalp. I lean over to stroke it, too, before dousing my hands in rubbing alcohol. I massage her calves until my hands burn from the heat between us. *All over,* she says. I move up the backs of her knees. Then up her thighs. She moans as if the pain worsens under my care. I notice the open door, and wish I had shut it. I find the creases higher on her legs and slide the sides of my palms in them, brushing along the lace hem of her nightgown. *Do you hurt all over?* I ask. *Yes,* she says, *even higher.* She quiets as I lift her nightgown and let it gather in the small of her back. She wears nothing else. I take her buttocks in my hands, knead them. I now know how soft and loose the skin of my own body will feel in thirty years. We have no words to travel through the walls, to wake up my sister so that she will walk in and see. Our mother, on her stomach, her gown hitched to her waist. Me, straddled over her body, about to collapse, on my knees.

Brooke Horvath

THE *ENCYCLOPAEDIA BRITANNICA* USES DOWN SYNDROME TO DEFINE "MONSTER"

> *humani nil a me alienum puto.*
> —Terence

I.

The encyclopedia's definition leaves my daughter holding hands with Grendel, the Cyclops, Frankenstein's monster, the mythic deformities of hell.

Chancing upon this definition leaves me face to face with the unspeakable.

II.

She is a monster who cries, recites with her sister the alphabet, has fallen in love with the boy at preschool who opens her yogurt for her.

She is a monster who meets with fear and stares outside and inside, holds the usual human emotions imprisoned by more than usual inarticulateness.

III.

My insurance company will not pay for her therapy. Therapy, a letter tells me, is covered only following an accident.

My insurance company does not believe in genetic accidents. My insurance company covers only human beings.

IV.

The *Encyclopaedia Britannica,* with its assurance that truth is tidy and knowable and human-sized, can shove its learning up its human ass.

It is anything human that is alien to me.

V.

My monster's favorite shirt has four hearts across its front. I ask her why she likes this shirt so much, and she points to the hearts.

You like hearts, I ask. But she shakes her head no, pointing again to each heart in turn and saying carefully: mommy, daddy, sister, me.

Holly Iglesias

THURSDAY AFTERNOON: LIFE IS SWEET

I know what's happening, see what's coming, and try like mad to fight it. Tapioca simmers in the dented pot. *The Joy of Cooking* says to use a *bain-marie* but I say, *bain-marie, my ass*. That Rombauer woman never shopped at Goodwill a day in her life. (He'll be home in three hours.) I stir constantly, watch carefully because that's what the damned book says to do but any fool knows that the stuff is done when the spoon starts to drag.

Tapioca has many lives, grows a new skin each time a scoop's dug out. Those beady little eyes—even though the cookbook insists on calling them pearls—bounce from the box all dry and nervous and then the hot milk leaches the starch out and makes a gluey mess. The book says, *Never boil the pudding*, but screw that: I love those thick, beige swells exploding like volcanoes, the sound as the surface breaks, the smell of burnt sugar at the bottom of the pot.

They tell you, *Spoon the pudding into individual cups,* but I put the whole mess in a plastic bowl and watch it quiver as it slides into the icebox. The kids like to press little dimples into it, then lick their fingers clean behind the icebox door so I won't know who did it. Me, I push clear through to the bottom of the bowl and my finger comes out so coated that it fills my mouth.

I leave the pot on the counter, won't wash it for hours. (*Slob*, he'll say, but I'm learning to ignore him.) The residue dries into a sheet as sheer as dragonfly wings and the kids will peel it off, laughing and drooling as it melts in their mouths. I can hear them yell now as they race up the driveway, pitch their bikes against the gate. The screen door slams and in rushes the smell of them: sweat, cotton, soap, candy.

David Ignatow

PROUD OF MYSELF

It's of no consequence to the grass that it withers, secure in its identity. I will take this thought into the world of elevators, crying, "Whether up or down, you are yourself always," and to a gunman, "You add nothing to yourself by pulling the trigger." The elevator rusts in its place, anxious, and the gunman replies, "I add myself to you, with this bullet." He fires. The victim falls. That's me, with a message brought from the woods. I am the message, watch me die, proud of myself.

David Ignatow

MY OWN HOUSE

As I view the leaf, my theme is not the shades of meaning that the mind conveys of it but my desire to make the leaf speak to tell me, Chlorophyll, chlorophyll, breathlessly. I would rejoice with it and, in turn, would reply, Blood, and the leaf would nod. Having spoken to each other, we would find our topics inexhaustible and imagine, as I grow old and the leaf begins to fade and turn brown, the thought of being buried in the ground would become so familiar to me, so thoroughly known through conversation with the leaf, that my walk among the trees after completing this poem would be like entering my own house.

David Ignatow

A MODERN FABLE

Once upon a time a man stole a wolf from among its pack and said to the wolf, "Stop, you're snapping at my fingers," and the wolf replied, "I'm hungry. What have you got to eat?" And the man replied, "Chopped liver and sour cream." The wolf said, "I'll take sour cream. I remember having it once before at Aunt Millie's. May I bare my teeth in pleasure?" And the man replied, "Of course, if you'll come along quietly," and the wolf asked, "What do you think I am? Just because I like sour cream you expect me to change character?" The man thought about this. After all, what was he doing, stealing a wolf from its kind, as if he were innocent of wrongdoing? And he let the wolf go but later was sorry; he missed talking to the wolf and went in search of it, but the pack kept running away each time he came close. He kept chasing and the pack kept running away. It was a kind of relationship.

David Ignatow

WITHOUT RECRIMINATION

It is wonderful to die amidst the pleasures I have known and so to die without recrimination towards myself and others, free of guilt at my shortcomings, happy to have lived and happy to know death, the last of living, my spirit free to sing as when I felt it born in my youth. The youth of it returns in dying, moving off from anger that racked its throat.

With death before me, I look back at my pleasures and they were you whom I held close in loving, and in the poems I've written for this truth, which is their beauty and lets me die in pleasure with myself. I did not fail my life.

Gray Jacobik

A LITTLE CHARADE

Every time I look up a school bus comes down the road. And huge white pieces of the sky keep falling in chunks on the lawn. The tough part about selling fish is your hands get raw. When we walked into the mist at the end of our tryst, it began to snow. She has an interview in North Carolina and another in Spokane and you know he's not about to change his job. Nothing as lovely as a primordial wood where mosses are ethereal and one sees the past by looking up, the future neatly through the trees. The boom came round and knocked him overboard; they called off the search after thirty-six hours. My mind's a calliope song, or a merry-go-round with canned calliopean music. The screen's flickering is a code and one day I will decipher it. Come with me little Rose, Rosy, Rose-of-Shannon the woman walking through the mall called to her three-year old. Oh Rose. Rose. Neither silence or its bell-clappered duplicate. When she'd been married a year she stopped moving through the world with assurance. Quail eggs around the windfall peaches. A gale tore across the island as if chastening the land. I'm happy to bend down and kiss his forehead and just to see his eyes. The electronic carillon got stuck in the middle of its six o'clock hymnfest; the one long sustained note felt paleolithic. He was a full-time street cleaner and she a full-time woman-of-the-night. Dandelion wine hasn't the color or the taste of dandelions and no one has ever tried to sell it, still I ask when I stop by the spirit shop, "Have you any dandelion wine?" The clerk smiles, or if he's young, calls back to the manager. I'm simply going to tell you what the imbecile said: *Forgiveness has teeth and those teeth are unpredictable.* Smiles all around, cascades of smiles. Splendid was her favorite word and then grandeur was and citrine is the stone she wants in her engagement ring. "Events," Durrell wrote in *Balthazar*, "aren't in serial form but collect here and there like quanta, like real life." Her ex-husband grew close to his ex-in-laws and joined their church, later began driving them to their medical appointments. I would not gainsay him for he's the experienced one. *Hat rack, coat rack, give me back my cane*, the children sang skipping rope.

Sibyl James

LE NOUVEAU TEMPS

The water's cut off again tonight. They must be digging on the new highway, working around the clock to paint white arrows, connect street lamps, at least on the strip between here and the presidential palace, so Ben Ali's black cop-flanked limousine can cut red ribbons on the new route on November 7th, the anniversary of the coup, the date of what the party calls *le nouveau temps,* the new time. They like to ring that date in with such ribbons, the paint on the latest metro stop or highway cloverleaf still dripping. Only the dark vans of police make continuity on every corner, the new time in the same old story. The stones in the graveyards head toward Mecca. On the roofs, the satellite dishes aim the other way.

Louis Jenkins

SEPTEMBER

One evening the breeze blowing in the window turns cold and you pull the blankets around you. The leaves of the maples along Wallace Avenue have already turned and whoever it was you loved does not come around any more. It's all right. Things change with the cycle of the seasons and evolve. A mistake, a wrong turn takes one elsewhere. But perhaps there are principles other than chance and natural selection at work here. Perhaps one changes merely out of boredom with the present condition. Perhaps our children, from a desire to become simply other than what we are, grow feathers, learn to breathe underwater or to see in the dark.

Louis Jenkins

YOUR BABY

Cry and curse, stamp your foot down hard, because the surface of the earth is no more than a crust, a bunch of loose tectonic plates, something like the bones of a baby's skull, floating on a core of molten magma: chaos and anarchy, the fires of hell. And as you've been told repeatedly, it's all in your hands. It's like the egg you were given in Marriage and Family class. "This is your baby, take care of it." So dutifully you drew a smile face on, then as an afterthought added a pair of eyebrows shaped like rooftops. It gave the egg baby a slightly sinister appearance. Then a friend added Dracula fangs and said, "See, it looks just like its daddy." "Let me see," someone said and someone else gave your elbow a shove.

Late at night. Where is your demon child now, as you sit dozing over the periodic tables, half expecting the police to call?

Louis Jenkins

THE WORKING LIFE

The job is a minor discomfort, like shoes that are just a bit too tight. Most of us go through our workdays mechanically without thinking about what we are doing. "Hello. Anybody in there?" Our minds are elsewhere. "Hello, hello," the burglar calls out. Nobody home. You've become part of the vast, undulating daydream, swaying in the breeze like prairie grass. The burglar breaks the pathetic lock, empties the contents of the drawers, pulls the books from the shelves . . . There's your whole life strewn across the floor. The burglar steals the t.v. and the stereo and in return leaves new Visa and MasterCards with your name on them. You won't know this until hours later. This time of year we go to work in darkness, return home in darkness.

Brian Johnson

SELF-PORTRAIT (KNEELING)

I pray that I continue to love the resemblance of things. When the rocks become human nipples, wheat becomes the spines of fish, the trees are a family of wooden kings, and the train from Istanbul arrives at noon, dressed as a bride, I have no questions.

I pray to the cinematic flame. It is a turn, a moment of uneasiness, the first time alone in a foreign country. The faces are strange and unto themselves, like the birds nested in their towers. I walk on the painted glass and watch the monks reading.

Before sleep, I stare at my name in the light. I search the mosaic for inscriptions. A group of musicians is visible in the center, with a goddess twisting her nearly translucent hair over someone lying on a bed. There is a carafe, and hills.

I am like mumbling in the woodshed, the prayer without name, or origin, I am similar to that. Like a horse neighing out its state of loneliness, the hunter looking for his wife's hand, the snowfall, the indifferent river, I am that.

Roman tombstone, pagan script, table, soul and screen: nothing is left to children. You emerge from the wood talking of miracles, thermal springs and fish-stocked ponds. And here is the oldest game: the sun putting on the robe, putting on the robe and leaving.

Brian Johnson

NIGHT-BLINDNESS

I'm aware of the nature involved in adding and subtracting you; in placing you on the table in front of me, and reproducing you, like a clipping, exactly from memory; in saying, "How are you?" and "Where have you been?"; in inviting you to eat with me on Thursday, but forgetting the bread; in drawing you from a knapsack that is not mine, in a country that is not mine, in a room overlooking the sea, where I have the power of sorting words, and call yellow Gold, and carpenter Charpentier; in mistaking the voices of birds for the voices of women in church; in being unable to recognize a sponge except when I touch it by hand; in playing games, and believing there are no streets in London; in knowing the nurses from the doctors because the nurses move in white dresses, white shoes, and they move silently; in naming a lemon by its smell, and a watch and cane by hearing; in keeping the rain out of the bottle; in seeing a beekeeper at the mouth of the hive . . . I'm aware of the nature involved in loving you, and much else besides.

Jim Johnson

THE THINGS A MAN KEEPS

The things a man now keeps in the cab of a pickup truck: friction tape, jumper cables, county map, dinosaur bones, pliers, coffee mug with Town Pump logo, so many legal papers, letters to be mailed, maybe a tumbleweed or two, and, as we sharply turned the corner by the fairgrounds, a box, a small sealed cardboard box that slid along the dashboard all the way to the edge, struck the windshield, and fell to my feet. *That's my dad,* he said.

George Kalamaras

THE PREPARATION OF BONE GLUE

I am walking the night streets of Paris, completely naked except for a pair of gray ragg wool socks and two giant moth wings growing out of my back. They are the black velvet green of a 1920's opium couch and open and close when moonlight surfaces and submerges back into a bank of clouds. Black antennae bend like dark wands in wind. There is not a star in the sky, only Venus, and I have the desire to look over my left shoulder and say the name of my mother three times softly, like throwing salt on a path of fallen red maple leaves. *Georgina*, I say. *Geor-gina*, I repeat more slowly, tonguing the night air with the exaggerated thrashing of a gold carp at the edge of a temple pool. *Georgina*, I clench once more with the strain in my turned neck and rush of blood from the bend. From behind me, a man with a leg cramp walks past, sclaffing the ground with his left foot as if tapping for water. He doesn't notice me but several yards ahead suddenly turns and calls me by name. *George Kalamaras. You're that vegetarian from Indiana.* I'm startled. *How do you know?* I ask. *It's the moth wings*, he says. *You've taken such good care of my moth wings.*

He looks like somebody's bald uncle, ready to play roulette on a Friday night in 1920's Paris. He has the crush of a rain-moistened cigar. He resembles a peregrine falcon, his nose hooking into river fog wafting up from the street. *But I don't know you,* I think to myself, afraid to hurt his feelings. Who is this man with the limp of a bird dragging a broken wing? *Yes you do*, he suddenly hears my thoughts. He peels off his falcon head and is a lion, mane matted with Kalahari sand. He peels off his lion head and is a Victorian woman, face controlled and withdrawn and gorgeous like marble above her tucks. He cracks the marble and is an owl, then a falcon again. *I'm Max Ernst*, he says. *You just don't remember because you haven't yet been born.*

I run to embrace him. It is so good to see Max Ernst again. My eyes well with river mist but suddenly begin to burn as tiny street pebbles and flecks of sand ease out of my tear ducts. He hugs me, gently tapping my moth wings, stroking them like two lost and returning dogs. *There, there,* he says. *Green*, he says. *Solidified light from fading gas lamps,* he says. *The twin swans of Breton*, he says. *A pair of beautiful opiated broccoli heads*, he says. *Mirrored spots on a tissue of René Daumal's tuberculous phlegm*, he says. I want to take them off, give him something real, something solid, tell him it's o.k. That they were never really lost. That like anything truly loved, they're his, even if for a while they weren't. That like gray-green morning glories they just close sometimes when the moon goes cold behind cigar-fate clouds. That like jaundiced skin, they sometimes shrivel to protect faint inner layers of epidermal light, the velvet flight of birds at dawn leaving a field as sudden shotgun fire, sparrows returning all at once to a telegraph pole at dusk. *We must prepare the glue*, he says. *Wrap the tubes from your bones to narrow your blood*, he says. *Sap the marrow into a laboratory glass through a rubber hose*, he says. *Place the coils directly on your skin*, he says. *The hot metal plate over your groin*, he says. *Lie you on the couch and coax starlight into your ears so you can hear the deaf man's symphony*, he says. *Stroke those wands and brush your wings to stimulate the juices and the pulp*, he says.

We walk hand in hand looking for a place to lie down to hook up the hoses and tubes and plates and to prepare the bone glue. I am still naked, and a drop of sperm oozes out of the tip of my penis, onto my left sock. It is warm and sticky, a drop that becomes a tiny puddle, then a small milky pool on the top of my foot. I think of René Daumal coughing phlegm in lotus posture in India in dusk. It stays there on my sock, collecting dust, insects, a bumblebee, a torn pink tissue. It is so wonderful to see Max Ernst again, after all this time, and after never having yet met. I inquire about my mother. *Is she a lion?* I ask. *An owl? A peregrine falcon?* And he tells me she will be a cloud, then a shadow cutting water out of a red cobblestone pebble in Zurich, then a grain of sand from the Kalahari, then a red ant in the Gobi, then a morning glory seed so blue it will have to be born in Chicago, where I will follow, screaming for breath on the south side at precisely 6:18 p.m. on a Monday on a December 3rd not too far from now. *The night air will be cold*, he says. *But you will be warm*, he says. *Inside where the omphalos blood will bathe your wings*, he says. *And your wands*, he says. *Which will be my wings and wands*, he says. *Which will open and close, close and open as your mother breathes you into each turn*, he says. *Which will then massage her vagina when you are born*, he says. *And ease her pain*, he says.

I am so happy, holding Max Ernst's hand, moved to tears, because I love my mother. Love the memory of the scent of her red maple leaf thighs. Love the taste of salt when I turn in any grocers to touch a tomato and recall the steam of her spaghetti sauce bathing my face when I would hunch into her pan. Love these wings now that I understand the shyness beneath gas lamps of the color green, the first light at dawn easing out of the throat of a freshly dead sparrow, of a fallen spear of asparagus before the coming of the killing frost. Love the gold gasp of a carp as it thrashes against a green marble floor, veins of stone familiarly cool like fresh fish blood but air oddly oxidized like sipping through gills a lock of burning hair. I am so happy, walking down the street with Max Ernst, hand in hand, because I love my mother. And because I love Max Ernst.

(after Edward Hirsch)

Paol Keineg

TOHU

In Memoriam Paul Quéré

From Keremma to Porz Meur. If I were I, I'd live happily in the horrible blue, far from all literature. Its lies, foremost.

*

Happy sound, oh to lie down on it, on a mile of sea and light. White bands, rearview mirror. Smell of privet and manure. Alleyoop, with love, sandals and hats gone with the wind. Let's run across the sand toward those blurry fishermen. How they lean into the wind, walking, and live the rhythm of tides.

*

At fifty, in one language, in another and yet another, I'm doing well, I'm doing very well. I no longer adapt. Subdued, futile, to make you kick at ruins. What do you say to the guys that head the pack? More light. And to those who bring up the rear and allow themselves to fall, fall again, and think divine thoughts?

*

Body within the law, bright birds in the sky of ideas. Down toward Kersioul, dog-roses, two lines by Kervarker written on the blackberries. The bay over there, sun thick as a callus, humming with work, heart of stone. What, no skipper in these waters? nothing but parody?

*

Near Kervrezel, which no longer exists. I turned on my toes to see what's left. The flies are modernizing.

*

The winter over, it's winter still. The blackbirds envelop us in songs that end badly. I had my heart set on hearing a thrush. My mother said: the winter was hard, the thrushes are dead. Do I hear right? come back, naive songs, country to drive one crazy. So much cruelty out of the towns, out of the mouths of people.

*

The trees, whirled high, touch the ground. I had written something else, but we've scorned them enough, the poor old folks, this winter sky in the midst of summer. Crack the whip; and the crowd, abused, will abuse. The sky all movement, black and grey, so quick the words come out by themselves. You think of what you have lost, you never get back.

*

By the tree trunk, the flagpole. Past master in leashing. By both ears. Hands bound by services rendered. They yield up work in sounds, on the dry side, slim. Are puzzled. Go howling past clouds dressed in red. Like warring wild boars. Like gusts that raise the dust.

*

On ignoble roles. On the failed death scene. Tongue of evil days. Have fought with, have left with. Now, and again, my name carries. My name of saddle, backbone, broad shoulders. The child I perhaps was did not see the night approach, nor the thieves. He left carrying on.

*

Did you see the sun embrace, this morning, the triumphal chariot of the slaughterhouse? Chicken coops, pig sties, always at the heart of our devotions. Soul turned to capital, with the last memories of childhood. Tomorrow is Caesar's. Today, in a glass eye, we follow open wars.

*

On the god of battles, no comment. On his reek, his athletic rump in a sweat, no comment. On his dealings, doubles and provinces, no comment. On his well-dressed kids in the first row, no comment. On their

124

pleasures, their laughs, no comment. On their games, their exquisite taste, their spirit of geometry, no comment. On their smartness, politeness, brilliant studies, no comment. On their kids' kids, no comment. On their screens and keyboards, their miraculous pictures, no comment. Normal road, penal code, no comment. On handsome chiefs, roundtables, unwritten rules, no comment. On their country before the law, the pursuit of happiness, natural borders, no comment. On our gods with their mallets, our obscure narratives, no comment.

*

Sail ho. Quite
undeserved, white or black,
it moves past.
A sea of storm and war
below our battlements.
Like a how of night
a dungeon hole.

Translated from the French
by **Rosmarie Waldrop**

Bill Knott

HOMICIDAL DOMICILE II: NIGHT OF THE NO-PAR

The desire to carve criminals up into one's family retains more room in us than the grease, the gold, the urine conversant with the flood: even the left hand's appraisers shun the right's buyers.

Thus my testicles have divorced but continue to share the same house, if only your penis was sharper it would cut the scrotum in two resolving this rental stumpage, this game forced yet deigned to wear the day-jar's view.

Where the righteousness of noon corrupts windows; like a name slanted to cry; floorboards that tweak earth: cult pepper, hurled by turban cameras, we grovel at sculptors whose heels punctuate our idol.

Glittering incidentals, hours in which towers swim off their own balconies, ah what stylites live atop our I's.

Mary A. Koncel

THE BIG DEEP VOICE OF GOD

That morning Tommy Rodriguez heard a voice, so he piled his family into the car and headed down the interstate. "Take off your clothes," he ordered after a while. And because Tommy had heard the voice, maybe the big, deep voice of God, they all obeyed, watched shirts and underpants fly out the window, twisting and turning like strange desert birds.

Around noon, Tommy's wife began to wonder. She hadn't heard the voice but thought if she did it would call her "Sugar." "Sugar," it would say, "your thighs are hives of honey, and I am the Bumblebee of Love." Quivering slightly, she pressed her left cheek against warm blue vinyl.

At home she often wondered too. There, on those late summer evenings, she leaned across the sink into still white clouds of steam and listened. Opening her mouth, she always took in more than air and water.

Tommy drove a little faster, beyond the vast and restless sand, a failing sunset, the tangled fists of tumbleweed. In the backseat, Grandpa whined, and Aunt Maria began to pee. Tommy closed his eyes. He was sure salvation was just one billboard or gas pump away, sure the voice was whispering now. "Drive like the wind," it was telling him, "like a wild saint in the Texan wind."

Mary A. Koncel

AFTER THE WEATHER

Yesterday a man was sucked out of an airplane over the blue tipped mountains of Bolivia. He didn't cry "Emergency." He didn't buzz the stewardess. He just dropped his fork, opened his mouth, and let the wind gather him inch by inch.

The other passengers agreed. This was real life, better than the movie or chicken salad. They leaned out of their seats, envying the man, arms and legs spread like a sheet, discovering raw air and the breath of migrating angels.

Below, an old peasant woman beat her tortilla. She never dreamed that above her a man was losing his heart. Perhaps she was a barren woman and, when he landed, she'd say, "Yes, this is my son, a little old and a little late, but still my son."

And the man, he thought of wind and flocks of severed wings, then closed his eyes and arched himself again. He didn't understand. His head began to ache. He understood Buicks, red hair, the smell of day old beer. But not these clouds, this new, white sunlight, or the fate of a man from Sandusky, Ohio.

Mary A. Koncel

EMANUEL ON THE TIGHTROPE

In this small corner, snow drifts higher than the last flock of swallows, and the wind beats cherry trees as if they were cheap tin drums. But 1,200 miles south, in the big city, a man sits on a tightrope, eating cheese sandwiches and watching a television strapped to his wrist.

His name is Emanuel, and, 600 feet above sidewalks and cigarette butts, lawn mowers and potted palms, he's no longer a man with a dozen lug wrenches and a weary blonde wife. He's the man on the tightrope.

I know the truth. Today, as I shiver again while another round of winter pounds on my front door, repeating, "You, you, you," I know that this man is afraid of the earth. I am sure of this as I am sure that sky and lake can freeze together, that February follows January like a well-trained mutt, and that this man too has shuddered in his sleep.

Emanuel blows kisses to the crowd below. "It's a dream," he tells them, "the dream of a real, everyday man." He turns away from the sun that drags itself across the horizon, straightens his shoulders, and waves two fingers as if they were his flag.

Up there, he is safe. Yet all over the earth, people are shrinking back. Wrapped and huddled, they think of Emanuel growing taller, his bare chest catching last night's drizzle of stars. "Hold on, Emanuel," we whisper through our clenched right fists. "Hold on."

Stephen Kuusisto

NO NAME FOR IT

The little scotophobia at the edge of the eyelid. It's music like Sibelius' "Swan of Tuonela"—a white bird gliding across the lake of the underworld—the tiny, bright speck of the eye submerged in a blackened pool where something electric stings like a jellyfish: the stored memory in DNA, a fear of the dark that hums like wind through a conch, air in the crack of a window. It's between blades of grass: the dew that keeps the crickets silent.

Itum, Egyptian god of the setting sun, worshipped at Heliopolis, city of sunlight, here's my offering: the magpies of Estonia, the blackest birds I know. And let me give you a human-headed wish, that you in turn will regard and fear the sunset which only you can see. May your sole companion be a desert god: cow-headed, thirsty as hell.

Mersegret, snake at Thebes, who guarded the desert tombs, to you I give a postage stamp of soil: my solemn geography of visual borders. And let's be ceremonious, let's go slowly into the thicket. The tongue is useless for talking. Let's feel everything with our skins.

Pluck the sistrum, swing incense, wave an ostrich feather. The fear of darkness is upon us. We need lustrations of water, offerings of meat, honey, oils, fruit, flowers. And here come delirious bees, fresh from their underworld hive, to graze at our stamens.

I want to open the canopic jars in which the Egyptians placed viscera, fit offering on the black shoreline of scotophobia.

I want to romp for joy with the jackal-headed gods. To hell with reverential shyness, Demeter with her eyes cast down, et cetera.

I want a hot, mathematical serenity, I want the blood of Mithraic sun worship where the priests looked at the sky too long and let out a solar bellow. Let's worship the ugly sun, the one we look at until we're mad. Let's slit the bull's throat.

The little scotophobia at the edge of the eyelid: a fear of the dark: devouring shade, a terrible, hungry fish. And the fish is the eye's true descendant. We must eat it before it eats us: cannibals first eat the eyes.

Eye of Tuonela, here is your swan, risen from the ice.

David Lazar

BLACK BOX

I want to fly in the black box; sometimes I want to live in the black box. The ones they keep on airplanes, the ones that are always found, always safe. Last week a small plane went down south of town. There was footage of wreckage, and the ages of the dead. It always looks like the same small plane, the crumpled toy in a forest. There is steam from the downed plane, or is it mist. Mist in the same anonymous landscape, pines or elms or ash, with the carnage long gone. Then they talk about the black box and uncertain circumstances. Nothing was reported. Communication stopped. A missing blip on a computer screen means people are dead on the ground. Sometimes the plane, if small, private, will not show up where it was supposed to land. Two days later, a woman will miss a business class, a man will miss a reunion. And almost immediately talk turns to the black box, that inviolable space with the last words, words streaming in as the plane was screaming down. And I think: if only they had been in the black box they would be safe now, they would have been saved. And I think: let the words lie crumpled on the ground, let the words be the ones who can't get out. And let them lead the saved out of the box, freed into life by the giant key kept only by agents from the agency. The lid is open, and there they are: aged forty-two, and twenty-seven, and nine, from Dayton, from Poughkeepsie, from Encino, smiling and shaking their heads that we could invent such a miraculous box. And how nice that the boxes have become so available, too, so affordable: for the car, the boat, the home. The black box can always be found, and we are always in it, and always safe, and we come out explaining; we know why things happened, we know we'll fly again.

Larry Levis

THE LEOPARD'S MOUTH IS DRY AND COLD INSIDE

Now I am drying my body, but carefully, as if it doesn't really belong to me, and won't last. And now that I see it, alone like this in the mirror, I think I'm right; it won't last. After all, does a stray dog feel permanent when you touch it? Does something as singular as this ant on my sill? Or if I admit that stray dogs and ants might have a certain anonymous permanence, why doesn't my white, bruised skin? It doesn't look as durable as my wife's reading glasses. It doesn't even look as if it will outlast some clouds I once saw. They were cramped into the sky of a child's painting, and looked as if the child forgot to include them, and then suddenly remembered and put in too many of them, as if to make sure of something.

Larry Levis

TOAD, HOG, ASSASSIN, MIRROR

Toad, hog, assassin, mirror. Some of its favorite words, which are breath.
Or handwriting: the long tail of the 'y' disappearing into a barn like a
rodent's, and suddenly it is winter after all. After all what? After the
ponds dry up in mid-August and the children drop pins down each can-
yon and listen for an echo. Next question, please. What sex is it, if it has
any? It's a male. It's a white male Caucasian. No distinguishing birth-
marks, the usual mole above the chin. Last seen crossing against a light
in Omaha. Looks intelligent. But haven't most Americans seen this
poem at least once by now? At least once. Then, how is the disease
being . . . communicated? As far as we can determine, it is communi-
cated entirely by doubt. As soon as the poets reach their mid-twenties
they begin living behind hedgerows. At the other end of the hedgerows
someone attractive is laughing, either at them, or with a lover during
sexual intercourse. So it is like prom night. Yes. But what is the end of
prom night? The end of prom night is inside the rodent; it is the barn
collapsing on a summer day. It is inside the guts of a rodent. Then, at
least, you are permitted an unobstructed view of the plain? Yes. And
what will be out there, then, on the plain? A rider approaching with a
tense face, who can't see that this horse has white roses instead of
eyes. You mean . . . the whole thing all over again. Unfortunately, yes,
at least as far as we are permitted to see.

P. H. Liotta

A POEM FOR AHAB

Tonight as I knelt down to take the wild face of the white cat named
Ahab into my hands, as he licked the salt from my palms, I found the
traces of blood on his teeth and on the rasp of his tongue which cannot
speak, speak, that is, in the way we know the morphemes of language.
The blood may, may not be his; it blossoms like a signature along the
smoothed-back fur around his lower lip. Maybe it's from the other cat,
perfectly black, who lives like Ahab's negative underneath the tongue-
and-groove planked level floor of this tiny cabin in the woods. Ahab has
felt his life invaded. He growls with the soft purr of menace. Some-
times, long into dark, they tear and claw outside, they hiss and spit like
two adversaries that have always hated each other. What can I make
of this? How can I blame them, when I am surrounded by messages I
cannot understand? Tonight in this town two old women die simply
because it's winter; in St. Louis some innocent asshole chucks a lantern
through a tenement window: three children and their mother, gone; in
Afghanistan, Iraq—or some place I haven't heard of yet—a canister
of VR55, chemical agent that implodes each lung, cuts off breath and
turns the veins of each unwilling victim to a rubbery jelly, lies on a
grainy hillside waiting for the thaw of spring; in the fertile delta of that
sad country we once named Vietnam, the green shock of hunger strikes,
whole families starve, and deaths go unreported. They are all denied—
and no one comes to invade our living rooms via airwaves, where the
disembodied Oxfam voice deliberately explains the inevitable and numb-
ing pain of kwashiokor, how through lack of protein, it stunts both physi-
cal and mental growth, brings loss of hair and swelling tissues. The
statistics of distance strike like a cold tangent:

Today I read in a magazine of a distant relative, maybe not so distant,
who coolly murdered his lover and then did his best to represent her
absence with a wellspring of grief, how he had taken her face and
then slapped it once and then again and then again against the blue tile
of the bathroom floor, how he had dragged her to the kitchen and sunk
the three-inch blade of an instrument used for peeling vegetables into
her breast, and then, almost lovingly, carried her still warm body back
to their bed, laid her back as if to sleep. I keep mouthing his name:
Liotta . . . Liotta . . . a strange and neutral signifier of practically

nothing, a name which is my name, of course. I keep thinking of how I rise each day from a cold bed to breathe the living fire and cannot separate myself from distance, how each day I step across the surface of a planet passing always thirteen-and-one-third-miles every minute, thirty-thousand-miles-more-or-less per-hour, elliptically displaced about a star three-and-one-half-million miles every week and each year we are only closer to hurling ourselves across the universe. Caught in re-flection, to pass so smoothly through a world that runs on and on like an aimless river that knows nothing more than it is being pulled, and must respond. And so tonight, as I knelt down to take the white body of the wild cat named Ahab into my arms, and wiped the blood from his mouth, as he returned my cool attempts at care with the cold indifference of his species, and as I heard the sullen grumble of the black cat's growl beneath our feet, I wreathed myself in space, and knew, and not so suddenly—the embrace is all I have to shock me into love. There is always something underneath the porch, behind the closed yet unlocked door.

P. H. Liotta

A BALKAN ODYSSEY

In *The Eye of Odysseus*, a film that reels from one immense preten-
sion to the next, the vapid apathy of the wandering hero, played by
Harvey Keitel, burns through celluloid as yet another Balkan oddity. A
man with no name, who speaks each line with all the authority and all
the dispassion of an ancient Greek chorus, he must cross the wilder-
ness in search of himself.

There is a point to this odyssey, of course, but no one, most particularly
the director, has a clue as to where it could be found, so why should the
audience look, or care? It's the Balkan disease—to drift with no pur-
pose. The frozen stillness of Albania and the fields of displaced Greeks
staring toward a distant homeland they will never find, the fog shroud-
ing Sarajevo as a small orchestra conducts the mindlessness of war, our
hero cruising the Danube on a barge that carries the dismembered re-
mains of a giant statue of Lenin, whose one arm extends in a threaten-
ing—now impotent—gesture to the West as thousands of orthodox Ro-
manians kneel and cross themselves.

Moments like these that go on for countless minutes, as the camera
gropes for every possible angle, to make the journey matter. God forbid
that our hero should speak, because when he does it is as though the
sky has opened and the air is filled with a sudden dead silence. He
means to find the three lost reels of the Manakis brothers, the first
Balkan filmmakers, and he drifts from Tirana to Bitola to Skopje, Sofia,
Bucureşti, Constanţa, Beograd. He finally confronts, of course, the
ruined Sarajevo, but by then we know his odyssey is hollow, that the
reels of film that play on the dark wall of the Platonic cave in a Bosnian
basement are blank, mere shadows of that other world.

Comrade, we have sold ourselves the rope and hang from its sentence.
Lenin was right, and his dismembered arm still points threateningly. The
barge with the modern Odysseus drifts through the gates of Scylla and
Charybdis, with Charon as ferryman. Nowhere does a film so richly
deconstruct itself and show our artifice as it does at midnight, at the
dark Balkan border, when the voice of the customs agent intones in rich
Serbian, *Who is on this ship?* And Charon replies, *No man . . .*

136

Our hero misses the point. He searches the Balkan wasteland trying to find one. He leaves a carapace of broken love affairs in his wake, each increasingly absurd. *I cannot love you,* he openly weeps at his first loss. *Not tonight, my dear. I have a date with Lenin's foot.*

Such is the cruel mystery of fate, the hard failure of art. When it can compare beauty only to itself with such feeble arrogance. When the people of Sarajevo deserve far better than anything that ever existed to describe such exquisite, anguishing loss. Nothing, and certainly no man, shall suffice. In the film's final reel, he speaks in the dark, lost among faces that are just a flicker of light, suffers Penelope to learn how he shall be known by the signs of their first love, from ages before. Madness and sorrow, no, not even these, can approach the rage they must feel.

P. H. Liotta

IN MELVILLE'S ROOM

His smile tells us that he thinks we're idiots. *It's our honeymoon* I say. *My parents sent us.* He calls his daughter from the back to mind the store and takes us up the creaking stairs to floors of tilting oak. A room: cramped as the berth of a ship, and a couch of interlocking antlers beneath a window which overlooks the dead Nantucket winter. We browse among the books, the odds and ends. Not much remains. But here the man became his words: the wreck of *The Essex* and the whale, the vision that trails beneath all mortal acts, what little there is to live on when the spirit of a place has died. *Seen enough?* We lie, tell him that we have.

Rachel Loden

CHECK-IN AT NÜRNBERG

He's back, liebchen, just like you always imagined it, checked in to the penthouse suite at the Bavarian Hilton. He's not in his room; maybe he's down at the pool. If you climb up to the roof and press your nose to the window, you can see that the place is filled almost to the ceiling with a vast assortment of electronic gear, piles of suitcases, wardrobes full of clothes, stacks of new purchases still in their store wrappings, and a few floral arrangements and fruit baskets that look like gifts. I wonder how much he tipped the bellboy?

All this seems to be in order. There is, to be sure, one odd thing: a cheap transistor radio, perhaps Japanese from the fifties, set like an afterthought on top of a thick, wet bath towel, and playing cheesy accordian versions of the Horst Wessel Lied and "I Had A Comrade." But our guy's casual—none of that Thousand Year Reich stuff this time, he's probably downstairs working on his Aryan tan and taking calls before his shot, next week, on "Nightline."

He's even left his sliding glass door open, proving he's got nothing to fear from anyone. Why don't you slip in right now and snag the radio—it was obviously intended for you, anyway—and carry it down to the pool, letting the last, feeble strains of "Deutschland Awake" be drowned out by the elevator's new-age muzak. Sure, he may pretend to be shocked at first, but then he'll laugh his inimitable laugh; and who knows, with luck, the two of you might really hit it off.

Gian Lombardo

DROUGHTMONGER

The young man's grandfather sat on the bench in front of the store. He must be the grandfather. He sounds old enough—his chest rattles with each exhalation. He sits with a stick in one hand. A knife's in the other. Every once in a while he slaps its blade against the stick. That gets my interest. I think it will happen then, finally, he'll begin to carve. May there be a bird spirit so the stick is grabbed by the tail feathers and may a finger catch itself under the curve of the beak.

But I don't want to look too closely. I don't want to jinx him. Towards midday the young man comes out of the store. He taps the grandfather on the shoulder. He takes the stick out of his hand and lays it on the bench. The old man starts to look up at him, but decides otherwise and looks down at the knife which the young man is now placing in its sheath. He lays it on the bench's armrest.

This young man wears a checked shirt and sets a plate of beans in the grandfather's lap.

He sits with a fork in one hand. In the other is a hunk of dark bread. He dunks the bread into the beans every once in a while and takes a bite. What gets my interest is the fork in the other hand. He uses it to swat flies away from his food. It looks like he's beating something down, or off, like something was going to jump off the plate. May there be a coyote leaping out of the plate at his neck, that takes his throat in its mouth. May the old man's fork slice into the animal's back, jam into its belly. May the plate fall to the ground. May twin paths of blood mix on the bench's pine slats.

I don't know if the grandfather remembers the sheathed knife sitting next to him. I don't look too closely. I don't want to jinx him.

Gian Lombardo

ON THE BIAS

I know a man who thinks a perfect day is one that's wasted. No, not that one is *wasted*—I wouldn't dare say such a thing—but one in which nothing is accomplished whatsoever.

No events. No one pile (no matter how great or small) moved from one place to another.

It would have to be a perfect cipher with no exclamation of some beautiful thing or with no adrenalin rushing through your veins in response to some horrific threat.

Not even a morality play, without the tiniest degree of allegory, without a cat that might represent something else (say, the kitchen door or the roof or the third person in a *ménage à trois*) in the grasp of an owl that may be a sign of something else, but not—certainly not—of any reflection of boredom with its hunger.

Gian Lombardo

IF WORDS HOLD STILL

There are days I have to introduce myself on the phone. It's as if I had to utter some password to gain entry into a club that had no members. I'll first say, This is your son . . .

Yes, my son, she replies. I'm not stupid. You think I'm stupid. My son's not stupid. She works like the Devil, my son.

Yes, *he* works like the Devil.

She works like the Devil. You don't believe me.

Other days it's like falling asleep reading a mystery novel and dreaming a whole new set of clues.

She says, The man came and got the thing. Know what I mean?

Other days she's hot it's so cold outside.

The white's too deep, she says, I'd broil. Am I wrong?

Robert Hill Long

SMALL CLINIC AT KILOMETER 7

It did no good, the mercy dream. The belief that famine's dry ocean of sand and wind could be diked by hundred pound bags of enriched flour, sugar, dried milk. The erection of surplus surgical tents across the river-border from the guerilla actions, the efficient arranging of cots, plasma drips, bandage storage, the effort to keep as many of the wounded out of the monsoon, out of the sun. No good, the slow resisting of rage, the kindly cupping of each hand in prayer while facing the shot-up outskirts of the town, as though to hold water out to a thirsty sniper, and see the rifle laid down, and water taken as a final covenant. When the red bandannas agree to lay down their rifles for sorghum and millet, then we see the ditch just behind the treaty table. In the hands of the all-mercifuls, hard currency and flexible guarantees to whoever would lay down his flaying knife and drink the clean water flown in on white cargo jets, and promise hand over heart to employ the knife to dig seed holes.

The President's wife toured the facility, laid a sunscreened hand on this forehead and that shoulder, five minutes were allotted for her clinic walkthrough. There were so many photojournalists trailing her, they could not help stepping on the hands of some of the stretcher cases laid in the tent aisle. They knocked over a tray of syringes and injectable vitamins onto the plank walkway, the boots on glass sounded like teeth breaking. The helicopters were landing, they had to hurry. One of them looked backwards, pulled out a wad of local cash and tossed it at a nurse, begging pardon.

Bring the boy forward now. Let Nineveh see the number of bones it will take to purchase truth. Tie him to the hood and tie the girl to the trunk and rear bumper, and drive each street of the old city's square mile. Under your breath repeat O King of the age, these are the names of the bones only. O King of larder and pantry and silo and freezer, swollen with drugs and cowfat. Whose decrees part the air like knives part yellow fat from bone's white. This was your son, this your daughter, every bone of them ready to dance for gladness at a feast, to run carrying good news west and east to the farm and the fishery. What is it to sit under the high awning, on a hill bearing your title, and watch the knives flash at either end of the valley? Is it to see your word remain bright through the dust of children running? King of sweetmeat, of custard and egg and white crabmeat. If strong hurt calms, then all your children will know peace to the very bone.

Robert Hill Long

DOING HATHA YOGA

Unroll the mat in the basement, tell myself *OK Go,* and lift my bulk into the shoulder stand: aiming feet overhead till they drain white like water-lotus roots strung up to dry. Come down, evolve through a bestiary of postures: belly-up fish, cobra swelling to strike. Hover through locust, through crow, stretch my neck to a swan's, my legs to a peacock tail; lick the salt from my graying ape-muzzle. Then relive the inventions of men: the bridge, the wheel, the plow, the shooting bow. Hold each pose for all the sweat it's worth, flushing each image with blood. After thirty minutes, salute the sun and gratefully sink into the corpse.

Read their poems aloud, use the force and stresses gathered from a life resolved to the high, dry divide of its middle years. *Don't let them see the icy rock, the few alpine flowers you're allotted.* Walk among the seated, deer-nervous bodies, touch shoulders lightly, the old mammal reassurance: *once I sprang through lowland woods, too, and scared myself.* Sit by one and say, "Show me the face you had before you were born." Pronounce her name, and nod, and ask, "How does a mountain teach a deer to sing?" Surprise her into the utterance that will revise her into a human, a poet. *But do not ask her to breathe the thin cold air you inhabit.*

If you can imitate deer, you can counterfeit human: you can buy Safeway foodstuffs, crossing off your list, steering the cart with your daughter hanging on its prow. You can prepare meals for strangers as though they are the only angels you will accommodate in this life. Your daughter and the daughters of friends, pick them up, drop them off, dance, mask-making, fairy magic parties, let them develop the talent for doing without you. Read the bedtime stories with faithful inflections, as the small blue-furred monster, the flightless bird, nasal and hugely naive. None of this is to be remembered. Not a single errand or shred of altruism, none of the consolings or funny voices, not a drop of sweat. Whatever falls to you, as inspiration or work or counsel or song, will fall away through the stone cracks, it's best to let it fall to the strange angels and animals below. *What can a divide do with its ice and snow?* I write on the blackboard. *Resolve it into water and air, and let it go.* "That's a heroic couplet," I point out.

Don was the name the newscasters used—I don't know what name his mother used. I used Don when I spoke to him. My teachings were good and Don was too far gone, or else Don was straining toward a zero-degree atmosphere above my resolutions of rock and ice. Which of these wrongs accounts for the pistol cocked and tucked under his chin? *If each day is a bullet,* he wrote, *each second is a grain of black powder.* His notebook was cross-wired with injunctions to purity, black and tiny as Bible sentences, and with vinings of insane metaphoric desire. On an empty page I wrote *We'd better make an appointment together.* But he didn't show, not as a deer or a swan or a patient student of mountains: instead, on TV, he showed me the blank face he had after he died. Oh, Don, this page too, and all the moves I made on it, is another exercise that ends in prostration.

Morton Marcus

THE MUSSORGSKY QUESTION

The Mussorgsky question is an intriguing one: Should he be taken seriously as a composer, or was he merely a talented dilettante? Balakirev said, "His brains are weak." Tchaikovsky considered him to be talented but concluded that "he has a narrow stature and lacks the need for self-perfection." Tolstoy dismissed him by saying, "I like neither talented drunks nor drunken talents!"

A heavyset man with a clown's red nose and eyes that seemed circled by charcoal, Mussorgsky was drunk much of the time and in the end lived in a single room strewn with plates of half-eaten food and empty vodka bottles.

No one knew, however, that Mussorgsky was Dostoyevsky's greatest creation. So great, he sprang from the novelist's pen full-grown— and very drunk—on a stormy night in 1839, when Dostoyevsky, dreaming of becoming a writer, was an eighteen-year-old student at the school of Military Engineering.

Yet over the next forty-one years, the author didn't know where to place Mussorgsky: he was too talented to play Sonya's father or any of the other drunks who stumble through the pages of Dostoyevsky's novels.

Nevertheless, the author never abandoned the idea of using Mussorgsky, and put him on the Nevsky Prospekt until he found a suitable part for him in one of his books.

As drunks will, Mussorgsky wandered away, bewildered by all the lights and jingling horse-drawn sleighs. He vaguely remembered that he was a minor clerk in the Department of Forestry and a former officer in the Preobrajensky Guards, but he didn't know how he came to be standing on that boulevard. Since he was a drunk, however, he went in search of the first tavern he could find to solve his confusion.

Like all Dostoyevsky characters, Mussorgsky was an idea surrounded by flesh and clothes, so single-minded and uncompromising, as ideas are, that he could never adjust to life. He had given up his army career to compose and lived only for music. Elegant, witty, perfumed and slim, he grew corpulent and shabby and would disappear for months on end, surfacing more disheveled and delirious than he had been before.

Periodically realizing that Mussorgsky was not where he had left him, Dostoyevsky would hunt him down and bring him home, making him wait in a straightback chair in front of his desk, while he sought a place for him in the novel he was currently writing. This would go on for weeks, Mussorgsky all the while sitting upright, licking his lips and looking moist-eyed around the room for bottles.

Other than physically, Mussorgsky was half-formed in every way, even in music, where his harmonies and structure were so "rough" and "wrong" they inspired Rimsky-Korsakov, Ravel and others to revise and rescore them in the forms we know them in today, although how much of the music is theirs and how much is this bumbling phantom's, who may have existed only as an uncomfortable but thrilling thought in their conventional minds, we will never know.

Dostoyevsky never used Mussorgsky. Those other drunks, Marmeladov and Snegirov, were minor figures who functioned perfectly as victims; sufferers at the hands of others. But Mussorgsky— Mussorgsky was special: he had the soul of an artist, and this Dostoyevsky did not know how to handle. Possibly Mussorgsky was closer to Dostoyevsky's character than the novelist dared to understand.

With the creation of Ilushia's alcoholic father in *The Brothers Karamazov,* Doystoyevsky stopped trying to find a niche in his books for the composer. He put Mussorgsky on the boulevard and, shoving him forward, he withdrew for the last time.

Mussorgsky was more bewildered than ever. How was a character supposed to behave who was created for a book that was never written? How was he to function? What was he to do? We can appreciate these questions, dear Reader, since, one way or another, we ask them of ourselves almost every day.

In the end, Mussorgsky composed three operas and a handful of song cycles and tone poems. All are poorly written. No wonder many consider him a dabbler in music.

Composer or dilettante? Is that the Mussorgsky question? Or is it about the model who inspired others to be better than themselves by being so single-minded, so dedicated to his art that alcohol was the only other thing that had a place in his life? His commitment was so uncompromising that he could never be believable as a character in a novel, or for that matter as a human being.

The Brothers Karamazov was published in December, 1880. Dostoyevsky died of hemorrhaging lungs on January 28, 1881. Six weeks later, on March 16, Mussorgsky, enfeebled and suffering from delirium tremens for the previous two months, died of a stroke.

Both men are buried in the graveyard of the Alexander Nevsky Monastery.

Morton Marcus

THE STONE FLOWERS

(for Donna)

There was a time when stones flowered. I need to believe that. In forests and fields, layers of black rock cracked open after rain, and slick pink petals swarmed into the wet sunlight. And those who saw this weren't astonished because such blossomings happened all the time.

As recently as the nineteenth century, miners reported seeing chunks of coal blossom with blue flowers as tenuous as flames. Some said walls of coal sprouted blue flowers all around them, and with picks at their sides they stood speechless at the wonder of it.

On the beach at night, I've seen the sand shimmer with a green phosphorescence. The next day I imagined the sand was acres of seeds, and I thought, "That's what this Earth is: seeds."

And when I look up at the stars sometimes, I think that's what this planet is, a seed hurtling with others through space.

When my wife weeps for our son or the death of a relative, I think of all the seeds scattered over the earth like unlit points of light lying gray and dull next to golden specks of mica and the glassed-in worlds of opal with their trapped swirls of celestial flame.

I know that the earth is full of cinders and hard seeds that have never blossomed, and that it makes no difference if pink flowers once surged from layers of black rock, or if one day the planet will crack open and shoot a pink and blue geyser into the night that will unfurl like a celestial flower.

I know that whether times are good or bad, we ride this planet like mites crawling on a pebble.

That is why I am not ashamed to say that flowers once blossomed from stone: I need to believe in every possibility. We all do.

Morton Marcus

THREE HEROES

1.

Zapata rode a white stallion. When it galloped, its tail and mane were clouds swirling into storms. And when it sauntered into a village plaza, everyone knew that the man in the saddle was no ordinary campesino: under the wide brim of his sombrero, the mud-brown eyes were of the earth, their earth, as if their anguish and anger and the sweat of their labor had taken the shape of a man who had come to avenge them all.

2.

The Baal Shem rode in a buggy tugged by a donkey. A big man with broad shoulders and ponderous belly, he was too large for the rig, but he rode in it over the rooftops of Eastern Europe, this tavern keeper touched by God, this confidant of angels, who was such a comforting thought in the minds of his people that when he clopped through a marketplace everyone nodded and smiled, so happy to know he was there that it made no difference whether he was on his way to wrestle the Evil One or to fill a grocery list.

3.

Sor Juana Ines de la Cruz slid through the covered walkways and sacred portals of old Mexico, the black hood tenting her head in the same way the black habit tented her body, as if she moved through a longitude of night containing continents and oceans. It was a night where plunging ships wrenched the knowledge of the past into the future, and where, here and there in darkened villages, specks of light, fluttering from the windows of earthen huts, identified solitary figures reading at candlelit tables, learning from the great books of the dead how to make life better for the living.

Peter Markus

LIGHT

When he wasn't working, on his days off, his father liked to spend his day outside, in the shingle-bricked, single-car garage, tinkering with his '52 Chevy Bel Air: a stoop-roofed, two-tone junker he bought off a drunk buddy of his, a fellow hot metal man by the name of Lester Litwaski, for a fifth of whiskey and a scrunched-up dollar bill. There were days when his father wouldn't take five minutes to come into the house to eat a hot lunch. Days like these his mother'd send him outside into the garage with a cold corned beef sandwich and an apple, and his father'd stop working only long enough to wolf down this food, his hands gloved with grease and dust, before ducking back under the Chevy's jacked-up back axle. Sometimes his father would fiddle around past midnight, his bent-over body half-swallowed by the open mouth of the hood, his stubby, blood-crusted fingers guided by the halogen glow of a single bare light-bulb hanging down like a cartoon thought above his hunch-backed silhouette. Sometimes he would stay up late and watch his father's shadow stretch like a yawn across the walls of the garage. And in the darkness of his room he would sit, silently, on the edge of the bed, by the window, and wait for that moment when his father raised up his hand, as if he were waving, as if he were saying good-bye, and turned off the light.

Peter Markus

BLACK LIGHT

For years he had heard his father talk about work, about carbon boils, tap holes, skulls of frozen steel. And he had spent many nights lying in bed awake, nights his father worked the graveyard shift, wondering what it all meant, as if the mill, and the life that went on inside it, was a part of some other world: a world he and his mother did not belong to. But one day all of this changed. One day he decided to ask his father if he could come inside, if he could go with his father to work, to see what it was like. And his father said he did not see why not, though he'd have to clear it first with the plant manager, a tie-and-shirt type of guy by the name of Russell Prescott. Which he did. And a date was set for that following Monday. And so, instead of getting ready to go to bed like he usually did at eleven o'clock, listening to the final innings of the Detroit Tigers game, the voice of Ernie Harwell drawling through the dime-sized speaker on his transistor radio, he found himself walking the quarter of a mile upriver with his father, step by step in the darkness of this mid-July night, the sky frosted fly-ash gray with a haze that hung over in the wake of the day's ninety-degree heat. His father didn't say anything the whole way there, though as they passed through the black-grated entry gates of Great Lakes Steel, he pushed his hand down into his front trouser pocket and pulled out two tiny tablets of salt: white like plain aspirin. "You think it's hot out here," his father warned. "Just wait until we get inside." And his father dropped the pills into his hand. It was true. Inside, the heat made it hard for him to breathe. The hot metal was so bright, it was so black with light, he could barely stand to watch as it drained from the blast furnace down to the thermo ladle waiting below. He closed his eyes, held in his breath. But still he could see the sudden flash of molten sparks showering down, could taste the burn of cooked limestone slag, could feel the callused hand of his father reaching out toward him, taking hold of him, turning him away from the light.

Dionisio D. Martínez

THE PRODIGAL SON IS SPOTTED ON THE GRASSY KNOLL

—again. The question would be moot but for the fact that a single bullet has generated so many overlapping and contradictory theories; it would have all been over long ago if we had not kept asking ourselves what are the facts in the fact. The crowd—the cold-blooded, stain-resistant crowd—is his weapon of choice. He is whistling "The Yellow Rose of Texas" to himself, but the song crashes into the slanting wind. This is found music at its corrosive best. John Cage might have called it accidental but necessary music; he might have said no composition is subject to the same interpretation twice, implying that written music is mostly not written and certainly never finished. Cage notwithstanding, his motive is yellow roses, tiger lilies in a tin can; it is the whistling itself.

Michael Martone

A VILLAGE

"Who dreamed us here?" the inhabitants of this village ask in their dreams. They try, upon waking, to renegotiate the covenants inherited from their ancestors—the dazzling hue of their houses, the shifting distribution of the neighborhoods. Their undreamed dreams accumulate, cloud the black, black night with sparks of color. They forget to ask. They ask. They forget they've asked. They ask. Who smudged out the road that was never there? Who erased the sense of a sense of direction? They dream: "Who dreamed us here?" "Did you?" they ask. "Did you?"

Michael Martone

A RESORT

Spring finds hundreds gathered here to stand for something else. The
participants remember to observe, and the observers remember to par-
ticipate! Everyone remembers to remember! A lock of hair becomes a
copse of trees; a fingernail turns into a placid lake. At the cocktail
parties, you are encouraged to sample canapés of your own fingers but
forget, until you remember, you have no way of picking up your fingers!
And later, they unfold the map! Its scale is 1:1! It corresponds exactly
and fits like skin! It is your skin!

William Matthews

TALK

The body is never silent. Aristotle said that we can't hear the music of the spheres because it is the first thing that we hear, blood at the ear. Also the body is brewing its fluids. It is braiding the rope of food that moors us to the dead. Because it sniffles and farts, we love the unpredictable. Because breath goes in and out, there are two of each of us and they distrust each other. The body's reassuring slurps and creaks are like a dial tone: we can always call up the universe. And so we are always talking. My body and I sit up late, telling each other our troubles. And when two bodies are near each other, they begin talking in body-sonar. The art of conversation is not dead! Still, for long periods, it is comatose. For example, suppose my body doesn't get near enough to yours for a long time. It is disconsolate. Normally it talks to me all night: listening is how I sleep. Now it is truculent. It wants to speak directly to your body. The next voice you hear will be my body's. It sounds the same way blood sounds at your ear. It is saying *Ssshhh*, now that we, at last, are silent.

William Matthews

ATTENTION, EVERYONE

Gloom is the enemy, even to the end. The parodies of self-knowl-
edge were embossed by Gloom inside our eyelids, and the abrasion
makes us weep, for no reason, like a new bride disconsolate in the
nightgown she had sewn so carefully. The dog comes back from the
fields, lumpy with burrs. I put down my pen and pull them out; it is a
care I have taught him to expect. I've always said it would be difficult.

I'm declaring a new regime. Its flag is woven loam. Its motto is:
Love is worth even its own disasters. Its totem is the worm. We eat
our way through grief and make it richer. We don't blunt ourselves
against stones—their borders go all the way through. We go around
them. In my new regime Gloom dances by itself, like a sad poet.

Also I will be sending out some letters: Dear Friends, Please come
to the party for my new life. The dog will meet you at the road, barking,
running stiff-legged circles. Pluck one of his burrs and follow him here.
I've got lots of good wine, I'm in love, my new poems are better than
my old poems. It's been too long since we started over.

The new regime will start when you lift your eyes from this page.
Here it comes.

Kathleen McGookey

DIFFICULTY IN MY HEART

Enough dogs and grace, enough feathers and gold, finally a way around the difficulty in my heart—I am small and sad and sorry. How it hurts, this managing a life. Yet people do. So there. So the man puts on his hat and walks out of the bank. The money is irrelevant, someone says. The woman puts on her green dress and goes to work, wastes her heart on envelopes and paper clips and the whole thing must be done again tomorrow and tomorrow, a sea of faces painted gold, a pointy sea of envelopes. Nothing as important as a small heart in the crowd, a mud puddle, the sun at the window. There's no rhythm in my feet or heart, just plodding—get it done, get it done. Maybe the money will pile up. Maybe not. I am walking in the glamour of my good health. Wouldn't it be nice to sleep a hundred years, wake dressed like a grandmother, safe to a degree in your own skin, and someone at your elbow? But I am not a beauty when I'm awake, with unappealing thoughts and insecurities. Will there be enough? If not? I have one wish and I wish . . . for everything to show its true colors, so the eye will be satisfied, the eye-teeth, but not my poor misguided heart.

Kathleen McGookey

Ugly, smiling Agnes with eight pearl buttons on her blouse; sad and lonely Agnes in the boat, afraid to venture out. She has an unfortunate nose and her bulldog clearly loves to have his picture taken. Agnes and her brother holding bunnies. She tries to salute my grandfather but the sun gets in her eyes. She tries to look fetching from a distance, from across the sea. She loved him, so she tries. At first I thought it was a matter of simply buying something shiny and new, a shirt in a bright color. But the heart wants what it wants. Right now my heart is sick and I am sad in January's good weather, rain and green lawns. Agnes looks pretty in a field of cut wheat, white dress and hat, black boots; she succeeds because she doesn't try too hard, she just leans into the scratchy wheat, not smiling. The wide open space becomes her, finally a place where the heart can be let free. Somehow she hasn't pictured herself here, ever, or her silent image in my hands, or the moon and trees speaking in a summer wind at night. She could be here, in the wheat, and it would be all right to be alone, maybe better. A woman in a dark coat holds two mules; not Agnes, and no way of knowing who, exactly, she is. And here's Agnes with a group up to their necks in river, smiling. The focus so sharp that everything looks hard. Then my grandfather and Agnes on a bench in front of the river with their legs entwined. She bends her head, already deferring. She wanted him then, got him just once: this photo.

Jay Meek

ROADSIDE MOTELS

I like to stop at motels built when tourists believed in cars the way they believed in safaris. There are motels steaming on the veldt, and motels shaded under the baobabs; some motels for the timid, and some for the assured. There are stucco motels where elephants pull in slowly, and motels for yaks, beatific and lascivious. There are family motels the wildebeests swim for, thousands of them crossing a river. Maybe an alligator strikes, or babies get trampled, but still the old bulls keep rising up the bank as if they saw the neon sign that spelled everything out: "Folks are Welcome Here." That's the roadside motel we're all heading for, clean rooms and cable TV where no one asks anything except an honest address, and where we can wake up the next day and look out at a field of antelopes grazing in the mist.

Jay Meek

LEAVING THE ROADSIDE MOTEL

A ventriloquist sat in his car and tried to start it, but it wouldn't turn over. He was in a dreadful fix to be going, and I asked if he needed a jump, but he didn't answer. He just looked straight ahead and ground on the starter. The others talked among themselves, back and forth over the seat, and as they posed their bodies a certain way, or held their heads at a familiar angle, I could tell these were famous people, most of whom were now dead.

The three in back were actors, and the woman beside him an actress who in real life had been beheaded in a car crash. They were each dressed according to the role that had made them famous on the screen. But as they continued to talk lightly about what I couldn't hear with the windows rolled down, I could see these were not the famous ones, but models who in some way resembled the famous. This was how near they had come, and how far they had missed by. As the driver turned the key, sometimes the battery sparked, and everyone lurched forward. When they did, an eyelash dropped from one of the women, or a monocle shattered, and one man in the back seat wept over the aristocratic nose that had come off in his hand.

I used to wonder what the ventriloquist's doll did at night, alone in its box, but I see now that it must have done no more than cherish the silence, a few hours without manipulation. And the ventriloquist, what does he feel, at a loss for words? Everyone is endangered.

Jay Meek

FORCES

On the Lake Shore Limited, a man behind me is talking about his trip, tracing the life of the birth mother he never knew. He says that she and his adoptive mother worked long ago at the same war plant, and when the man speaks he names cities and streets, as if writing the obituary to a vigorous and articulate life. I can't follow the whole story, except it's clear that he has gone looking for her, for some part of himself. He is crossing the country, mapping the woodlots and rivers that make up his life. Who can be listening, so empty and silent? At times, when the riders across the aisle begin talking, I can't make out the man's words, and by the time they stop, I have missed a new deposition, some further enchantment.

Nights in my apartment near the freight yards, I hear rims grind against rails, steel on steel, as the dark gondolas pass. Of force, Leonardo says, "It is born in violence and dies in liberty." He's talking about the power that turns people to stone. "Speed," he says, "enfeebles it." On the train in Massachusetts I hear him. In far North Dakota I hear him. For I have seen men in exercise rooms, walking beside me on the treadmill, step for my step. Mornings we work out on the arm curl and shoulder press, or rest on the rowing machine with towels around our necks, men like me who are gearing up, with the sun darkly risen.

Now, riding coach, I follow the Westfield River, which at times cuts away into deep woods and at other times rushes under a bridge we quickly cross. It's early morning, fall light in the trees. Yesterday, waking on a new campus, I looked out my guest room at children holding hands: two on two, on either side of their teacher—the children bumbling on, small and large—children of color and of pale skin—all of great wonder, walking with their teacher across the college green.

Christopher Merrill

FROM *NECESSITIES*

Return the swastikas—that's what the letter instructed us to do. There was no signature, although the canceled stamp bore the figure of a famous poet. The thieves thought our confusion was a mask. Nevertheless they offered to forge new documents for us. Our passports had expired, and we were afraid to ride our horses over the Alps—the Trinity Alps, that is, where vigilantes had turned the sawmills into training centers for the afterlife. The felled trees spiked with nails, the tribes drowned in the lake, rugs woven out of feathers: these we could return, at least in theory. Where's the poet now? we asked the thieves, who were printing up a series of manifestoes concerning the rights of bears. We had run out of fences. Feathers, too. The horses lay on the ground, in the first snow of the season. We propped a cross against the barn door and bolted it shut. We vowed not to open our mail until the spring runoff, when we could present our credentials to the guards at the pass.

***

Every building from the century in which costume balls prevailed must be razed, according to the professors of desire, the men in top hats writing letters of recommendation for their versions of the past. The wooden matches they produce will never light the stove or end an argument, though the warm waters leaking from the canisters in the salt caverns should clear our minds: every marksman can see the river glowing at dusk. *Razed* or *raised*? These are terms only the initiated employ. But no one will go hungry tonight, at least not in the canyons patrolled by coyotes. Fill our wine glasses with Apache tears, hard and black as the forgotten histories of America: we would use them as instruments of writing or torture, if we weren't afraid of the dark. Nor can we console the woman crying by the stove; the dress she bought at an estate auction is stained with blood. Besides, say the professors passing their top hats out the window, it's too cold to wear a sun dress to the ball.

***

Reinvent the past: that was how the patent lawyers proposed to solve the housing shortage. Resurrect the sonnet and symposium, crossbow and convent. They filled prescription pads with demolition orders for the illiterate. They watched the river burn. The drunken ferryman suspended all crossings in calm weather. No passengers complained when the inventors, who preferred to work in their sleep, promised to march one night with the homeless, whose protest was in its seventh year. The ground was shaking again. Bridges crumpled like paper. *Sell today, or jump tomorrow!* was the cry we heard outside the stock exchange. The futures market had closed early, the fire having spread from the mouth of the river into the songs of the women in the street. No one said a word about the man carrying a rifle into the patent office: he looked like any other soldier of fortune. Even when he took aim at us we held our tongues. Sunlight streamed in the window. We smelled smoke.

***

The blacksmith speaks in tongues to settle the horse that kicked him in the head one night, the white mare he must shoe before the exodus begins. The metal place in his skull functions as a lightning rod for the church; his congregation thinks the rusted nails he uses once belonged to a saint. But no shoes fit; the fire keeps burning out; and the horse's owner, who paid in knives last time, forgot to enclose enough pennies to ward off bad luck. The boatload of refugees who drifted out to sea, believing the new anchor would catch, have thus returned to port. *A word is a rudder and a sail*, the blacksmith sings to them. *Where will we sleep tonight?* they ask. He tells them his dream: to forge a currency out of alms and intrigue. The horse is impatient. Likewise the faithful marching toward the paddock, scanning the sky for thunderheads, the ground for nails. In the barn is a cross soaking in gasoline: if the blacksmith's luck changes, one spark from his anvil will ignite another wave of conversions.

Henri Michaux

SIMPLICITY

That's what's been missing from my life: simplicity. Slowly but surely I'm beginning to change.

For example, these days I never leave my house without taking my bed along. If a woman passes by and catches my eye, I take her to bed immediately.

If her ears and nose are ugly or too big, I remove them along with her clothes and put them under the bed, ready for her to take back when she leaves; I keep only what I like.

If she could use a change of undergarments, I arrange it. It's my gift. If, however, I see a prettier woman walk by, I voice my regrets to the first and poof! she disappears.

Some people who know me claim that I can't do what I've just described, that I haven't got the balls. Well, that may have been true in the past, but that was when I wasn't doing everything *exactly the way I like it.*

Now I always enjoy my afternoons. (Mornings I work.)

Translated from the French
by **David Lehman**

Henri Michaux

PLUME HAD A SORE FINGER

Plume's finger felt a bit sore.

"Maybe you should see a doctor," said his wife. "Often it's just a matter of some lotion. . . .

Plume took her advice.

"Take off one finger," said the surgeon, "and everything's perfect. With anesthesia, the whole thing takes six minutes at the most. And, since you're a rich man, you really don't need so many fingers. I'll be delighted to do the operation, and then I'll show you several sorts of artificial fingers, some of them truly exquisite. Oh, maybe a little expensive. But of course expense isn't really an issue here, not when we want to provide you with the very best."

Plume, looking wistfully at the guilty finger, humbly objected:

"Doctor, it's the index finger, you know? A very useful finger. As a matter of fact, I was just about to write to my mother. I use my index to write. My mother would be anxious if I put off writing her any longer. I'll come back in a couple of days. She's a very sensitive lady, easily shaken."

"It's nothing," the surgeon told him. "Here's some paper, some good white paper, without any heading at all. Just send her a few reassuring words and she'll be happy as ever. Meanwhile, I'll be calling the clinic to make sure everything's ready: all they'll need to do is sterilize some instruments and pull them out. Back in a moment. . . ."

The surgeon was back almost as soon as he'd left, saying, "Everything's set. They're waiting for us."

"Excuse me, Doctor," said Plume, "but you can see how my hand is trembling. It's all too much for me. . . ."

"Yes, yes," the surgeon replied, "you're right. It's best not to write your mother at all. Women are so touchy, and mothers most of all. They're always picky about what their sons are up to. They make mountains out of molehills. You and I, we're never more than their little darlings. Here's your cane and here's your hat. There's a car waiting for us. . . ."

Soon it's the operating room.

"Doctor, listen! I mean, really. . . ."

"Quit worrying!" the doctor exclaimed. "You have so many scruples!

We can write this letter together, if that's what you want. I'll think about it while I'm doing the operation."

Fixing his mask to his face, he put Plume to sleep.

"You might've asked me for *my* opinion," Plume's wife said to her husband. "Don't think that a lost finger is something you can easily find again. A man with stumps? I'm not too happy with the idea. Once that finger's chopped, don't count on me anymore. I mean, cripples turn evil; they get sadistic, and I wasn't raised to live with sadists. I guess you thought I'd be a saint, and see you through the whole thing. Well, you were wrong, and you should have thought about it all beforehand. . . ."

"Listen," said Plume. "Don't make a big fuss over the future. I've still got nine fingers, and your character may change, after all."

Translated from the French
by **Sydney Lea**

Gabriela Mistral

THE FIG

Touch me: it is the softness of good satin, and when you open me, what an unexpected rose! Do you not remember some king's black cloak under which a redness burned?

I bloom inside myself to enjoy myself with an inward gaze, scarcely for a week.

Afterward, the satin generously opens in a great fold of long Congolese laughter.

Poets have not known the color of night, nor the Palestinian fig. We are both the most ancient blue, a passionate blue, which richly concentrates itself because of its ardor.

If I spill my pressed flowers into your hand, I create a dwarf meadow for your pleasure; I shower you with the meadow's bouquet until covering your feet. No. I keep the flowers tied—they make me itch; the resting rose also knows this sensation.

I am also the pulp of the rose-of-Sharon, bruised.

Allow my praise to be made: the Greeks were nourished by me, and they have praised me less than Juno, who gave them nothing.

Translated from the Spanish
by **Maria Jacketti**

Fred Muratori

FROM *NOTHING IN THE DARK*

        The blonde took her teeth out of my hand and spat my own blood at me. In isolation, an almost incomprehensible sentence, courtesy of Chandler, but a story in itself. And what about the eerie grace of *The woman stood up noiselessly behind him and drifted back, inch by inch, into the dark back corner of the room.* Not perfect, almost if not certainly ruined by the repetition of *back*, but in life I have often witnessed such imperceptible edging, sometimes by women, often by men. Guilt is no different retreated from than withstood. That's a Philip Larkin line in its bones. He was just a surname away from Marlowe, and would probably have been quite good at this game: nondescript, unmarried, few friends, his hand quick to the gun-drawer at the suggestion that routines he had spent a lifetime perfecting were about to be disrupted by a livid husband, or a beautifully enraged widow.

Fred Muratori

FROM *NOTHING IN THE DARK*

        In another life I might have been a songwriter. Sad, solid stuff, but the kind of songs that people remember in times of extreme emotion, the kind that break into the consciousness as if they were attempting a courageous and timely rescue, not changing or reversing the situation, no, but making it seem to make sense for a few seconds, since things that make sense aren't so terrible after all. Oh sure, you say, of course; it had to be this way. Why didn't I realize it sooner? Then the song fades, and the temporarily drugged emotion comes back, groggy and lumbering, and angrier than before, knocking over the expensive furniture in your cavernous heart, heading toward the fireaxe in its glass, unfingered case. Those kinds of songs.

Pablo Neruda

THE KEY

I lost my key, my hat, my head! The key came from Raul's general store in Temuco. It was outside, immense, lost, pointing out the general store, "The Key," to the Indians. When I came north I asked Raul for it, I tore it from him, I stole it in the midst of fierce and stormy winds. I carried it off toward Loncoche on horseback. From there the key, like a bride dressed in white, accompanied me on the night train.

I have come to realize that everything I misplace in the house is carried off by the sea. The sea seeps in at night through keyholes, underneath and over the tops of doors and windows.

Since by night, in the darkness, the sea is yellow, I suspected, without verifying, its secret invasion. On the umbrella stand or on the gentle ears of Maria Celeste, I would discover drops of metallic sea, atoms of its golden mask. The sea is dry at night. It retains its dimension, its power, and its swells, but turns into a great goblet of sonorous air, into an ungraspable volume that has rid itself of its waters. It enters my house to find out what and how much I have. It enters by night, before dawn: everything in the house is still and salty, the plates, the knives, the things scrubbed by contact with its wildness lose nothing, but become frightened when the sea enters with all its cat-yellow eyes.

That is how I lost my key, my hat, my head.

They were carried off by the ocean in its swaying motion. I found them on a new morning. They are returned to me by the harbinger wave that deposits lost things at my door.

In this way, by a trick of the sea, the morning has returned to me my white key, my sand-covered hat, my head—the head of a shipwrecked sailor.

Translated from the Spanish
by **Dennis Maloney** and
Clark M. Zlotchew

Kristy Nielsen

SELF-PORTRAIT AS MY FATHER

What does it take? I know how to wire a room, to stop an elevator in flight, to go hunting and bring home a puppy instead of a dead duck, I know when to lick the syrup off the plate and when to set down my knife and clean my teeth with a toothpick and listen

so talk already, tell me all about yourself, every little thing

I could tell you a story if you want to hear your old man ramble. Once there was a girl who couldn't cry no matter what and she grew to be a woman with buckets of tears inside, a huge woman who shook the ground when she walked and trembled the trees, a real fatty fatty two by four—can you hear me? You got potatoes in your ears? Scrub harder spud farmer

and listen up because it gets really funny. One day the woman goes walking in the woods, trips and falls across a stream bed, blocks the water, creates a dam, the water swells and pools and everything washed downstream piles up against her, trees and shoes, beer cans, shopping carts, parts of cars, waterlogged stuffed animals, amazing, all this stuff you didn't think was around anymore

all surrounding this woman who couldn't cry. She asked to be left alone so she could die, but instead the people came and took pictures.

Naomi Shihab Nye

HAMMER AND NAIL

"Would you like to see where our little girl is buried?" my friend asks as
we walk between stucco shrines and wreaths of brilliant flowers. Even
a plane's propeller is attached to a pilot's grave as if the whole thing
might spin off into the wind. One man's relatives built a castle over his
remains, with turrets and towers, to match the castle he built for his
body in life. If you stand at a certain angle you can see both castles at
once, the bigger one he lived in off on the horizon. An archway says in
Spanish, "Life is an illusion. Death is the reality. Respect the dead whom
you are visiting now." We hike down the hill toward the acres of "free
graves." Here people can claim any space they want without paying,
but also risk having someone buried on top of them. In the fields beyond
the cemetery, women walk slowly with buckets slung over their shoul-
ders on poles. Black cows graze on knee-high grass. The crossbar
from the marker to my friend's child's grave has come loose and lies
off to one side. My friend kneels, pressing the simple blue crossbar
back into the upright piece, wishing for a hammer and nail. The cross
has delicate scalloped edges and says nothing. No words, no dates. It
reminds me of the simplicity of folded hands, though I know there were
years of despair. My friend says, "Sometimes I am still very sad. But I
no longer ask, 'What if . . .?' It was the tiniest casket you ever saw."
On the small plots in either direction, families have stuck tall pine branches
into dirt. The needles droop, completely dried by now, but they must
have looked lovely as miniature forests for the first few days.

Naomi Shihab Nye

LA FERIA

Here comes the woman who never looks up with one little girl riding her hip in a shawl and one slinking alongside. The man who fathered these babies is hard to find. He is usually sleeping with the woman he loved before this one who doesn't feel bad about it because she had him first. He is ugly but creative. He has designed buildings in town no one wants to enter because they feel heavy. The first woman says he will marry the second one sooner or later and that will be fine with her. If he says it is time. When the little girls ride a carnival car at La Feria they grip the steering wheel tightly and don't wave. All the other children circle round and round, smiling as the tiny breeze ruffles their hair. They are going on long trips, they say. But these two look grim as if they are staying in one place.

Nina Nyhart

GHOST TRIPTYCH

My mother's not dead yet, only wandering, not knowing if she's in one place or another. So she comes to sit beside me easily, more easily than in the past. And she disappears easily, as she often did. As I drive along, my mother's ghost flinches, shrinks from the savage traffic. What can you expect, I say, we're in Boston. Stoplight. She squirms impatiently. I remind her how lucky we are to be together, here, after so many years apart. She grows silent, and finally, as if love were the result of an algebraic equation she must work out, she agrees.

*

My father's ghost often visits my mother. He spends afternoons with her talking over the old days. He finds her no matter where she has wandered to—Philadelphia, the Gulf Coast—and today, on shipboard. Don't worry, she tells me over the phone, the ship is tied securely to the dock, and someone is cooking dinner. She's growing cold, though, the ship's in Alaska now—serious fishing—and so many men washed overboard. Such a harsh life, fishing.

*

I go to starlight as to a beautiful woman, my mother, wearing a long white silk jersey dress of the thirties, Hollywood style. She sits at the skirted dressing table before the triptych mirror combing her dark wavy hair. Three women open their lipsticks, apply crimson to their lips, dab Nuit de Noël on their throats. She puts on her diamond pin and earrings all shaped like stars. They sparkle in the dark room— starlight—and when I reach to touch it, it's gone, back into that darkness she shone from for a few minutes, long ago.

Nina Nyhart

WAR STORIES

A man makes miniature soldiers and sailors, ship models, an array of tiny weapons. When his health fails, his wife takes over the business, casting the molds, painting figures, filling mail orders. The man is in pain and short-tempered. When the wife makes an error—she has trouble telling the guns apart—the husband yells at her: Stupid woman! The ships rock and the little men quake. The cannons and swords and bayonets, the Gatlings, Lugers, Derringers, and Remingtons lie in rows, poised.

*

How clear Picasso was that war is chaos—explosives falling from the sky, body parts flying. With the Guernica success behind him he went on fracturing the given. Pulling hair was just a start. What a kick to stretch a smile, to disappear an eye. A charming face bordered by curly hair, on a plate.

*

She was thinking of "historical precedent" and reading reports of the disintegration of a certain nation state—tribal wars, atrocities. Learning of the current barbarisms—mass rapings, giving knives to prisoners and ordering them to cut off each other's genitals, nailing children to doors—she was reminded of hearing that, in a former war, in another country, soldiers nailed horseshoes to the feet of their prisoners.

Tommy Olofsson

CHICAGO

Having followed an instrument maker to a Chicago slaughterhouse
and stood at the end of the conveyor belt picking out pieces of bone
suitable for harpsichord keys, and having subsequently grasped
Emerson's transcendental points about Aquinas and his scholastic break
with the accepted and (in the literal sense) metaphysical problems of
the resurrection, I want to propose herewith, in ample time for the
next assembly of churches, a memorandum concerning cannibals and
animals. Considering that cannibals are now a dying race without suf-
ficient access to their traditional diet, we should, as a deterrent and
also for the sake of ethnological research, make life easier for the
few tribes still hanging on by the skin of their teeth outside the aegis
of the Church. The situation of domestic animals is less precarious,
but they don't want to be turned into food and have actually never
chosen to be served on our plates. Pigs are slaughtered under protest
that squeals to high heaven. They want to go back to their fetid stalls
and wallow in the mud and await eternal life, which by right ought to
be available even to them. The pig wants to be pieced back together
again, to be made whole again so he can scratch himself happy against
a rough board. And the velvet-eyed veal calves crammed in their
crates dream of being granted just one glimpse of the sky's blue face.
Most of all they want to live forever, exactly like us!

Translated from the Swedish
by **Jean Pearson**

178

Imre Oravecz

I REMEMBER CLEARLY

the first time you came, you wore a short skirt, a transparent blouse, light sandals, your luggage was light as a feather, and you too were somehow light as a feather, sunny as the spring you came in, wide-awake, responsive to everything, and youthful, almost a child, and your body too almost a child's, downy and fresh, you told me in detail what the passport and customs inspection was like, what scenery you saw from the train window, how people treated you on the journey, and what it felt like to be in the *eastern bloc* for the first time, and you were surprised at what to me was unexceptional, and you found unexceptional what I was surprised at, you liked the city, you liked the old villas, the streets, the bridges, the confectioneries, the museums, the swimming pools, the police uniforms, the streetcars, and you tried ardently in bed to make up for what you missed in the meantime, and you always saw to it that I was pleased with everything, because you were pleased with everything, and you delighted in everything, in me, in yourself, in the world, and I remember clearly the last time you came, you wore a long two-piece suit, a bulky sweater, a pair of walking shoes, your luggage was heavy, and you too were somehow heavier and overcast as the fall you came in, withdrawn, already indifferent to certain things, and older, a real woman, and your body too a real woman's, mature and tired, you made no mention of what the passport and customs inspection was like, what scenery you saw from the train window, how people treated you on the journey, and what it felt like to be in the *eastern bloc* once again, you were no longer surprised at what to me was unexceptional, and you did not find unexceptional what I was surprised at, you were indifferent to the city, unmoved by the old villas, the streets, the bridges, the confectioneries, the museums, the swimming pools, the police uniforms, and you no longer tried so ardently in bed to make up for what you'd missed in the meantime, and you did not always see to it that I was pleased with everything, because you were no longer pleased with everything, and you no longer delighted so much in everything, in me, in yourself, in the world.

Translated from the Hungarian
by **Bruce Berlind**
with **Mária Kőrösy**

Robert Perchan

GILLAGAIN

Perhaps the most erotogenically exciting event a man can experience
in life at sea is to steam into a port city known chiefly for its whores.
They say Robinson Crusoe constructed a row of brothels out of palm
fronds and floatsam futtocks and jetsam jibbooms and waited for the
hookers to sprout out of the compost of his memory like mushrooms in
a cave. When that didn't happen he sat down on a palm stump and
wrote out *Moll Flanders* in a longhand so elegant it slithered right by
his self-censor. One night he even arrested his very own person for
indeliberate behavior—using his nom-de-sûreté, Clouseau (Thank you,
my love Miss Kim, for the Asiatic pronunciation cue)—and stood up at
his trial and, in a cursive self-headlock learned on the stocks, read from
the text of himself. This made the book the most popular on the island
and bathed him in glory. Even the cannibals loved it once he taught
them to decipher, though it did little for the repute of white women in the
Third World, where they are generally regarded with a fear and awe
akin to that accorded them in the First World only by their British and
American mates. Crusoe called Moll his heroine but the savages all
labeled her a slut, loitering around the futtock-frond-jibboom stews wait-
ing for her to show up, much as I hang around the apartment and wait
for Miss Kim to pop naked and glistening out of my brain like Athena
unarmored. It's the steaming into port that's exciting, I said, balanced
here on the slick fo'c'sle of my fancy like Lem Gulliver on Glum-
dalclitch's Brobdingnagian mons, a Little Man in a Freudian Boat, re-
membering Marseilles.

Robert Perchan

BACHELORHOOD

Mine began the year I divided all female living beings on earth into two types: those that lay tiny eggs in food, and those with better manners. At the Taxonomy Awards Ceremony I was given a suit of children's cheeks and babies' butts all stitched together like a pink quilt. But the children's squeals and the babies' farts hadn't been tanned out of their hides, and I made a hell of an undisciplined racket whenever I stood up and sat down or simply shifted in my seat. *Wah-wah-wah! Poot-poot-poot!* All day long and into the night. I smacked them as best I could, these children's cheeks and babies' butts, first with the palm of my hand and later with a penitent's scourge. But they only howled the louder, farted with greater acrimony. Finally one weary day in the middle of my life I stopped dead still in my tracks. And listened. And patted my suit soothingly. I wanted to understand. Still they yowled and still they spat bowel wind. But not like children or babies anymore. Rather, geriatrically, to be precise. My suit had grown wrinkled and threadbare from so much standing up, so much sitting down, so much smacking and scourging. Old already! Had I only married when I was young and had the chance—a broad-beamed maternal Brunhilda with a clothes wringer in one hand and a flatiron in the other. Someone who really understood her way around the pink suit of innocent flesh a man must bear.

Robert Perchan

NIGHTS AT THE RACES

He believed in a kind of metempsychosis, a transmigration of souls, that when he made bareback love to a woman in the solitude of his cabin all his dead male ancestors would show up and gather around the bed to cheer on the sperm carrying their own personal code. In the mornings the place would be a mess, littered with tote-machine tickets that had been ripped in half and the butt-ends of fat stogies that had been dropped or tossed away during an exhilarating dead-heat finish. And, sometimes, when he and the woman swept up, they would come across one of last night's losers, some dimly-remembered black sheep, some dead-end lush who had died without issue, huddled in a corner under an overcoat stained with vomit. And then, with charity in their hearts, he would don a condom and they would slip back under the blankets and knock one off just for suchlike lost souls, the unbegetters, the true wand'ring Shades, the eternally stopped.

Jane Lunin Perel

BLOOD SOMEWHERE

Carnelia does not know what to think of the world-renowned Doctor on whose office walls glide eight striped, wooden fish with aluminum eyes and cork pupils. Fish with chrome tails. They swim like zombies whistling voodoo tunes. They are next to the eight black and white prints of rotting cauliflower, across from the mandala of hemp and dried blood. "Did you have the blood somewhere else?" the receptionist asks over the phone. Did someone lose her blood, Carnelia wonders, or store it in an unsafe place, a refrigerator in a slum that Dobermans snarl at? The door to the office is solid mahogany, framed in black. The handle is chrome that shines like a scalpel. It's supposed to calm you, these off-white walls, this recessed lighting, this black leather seating, but Carnelia thinks that if she stands up and walks to the door, opening it, a zebra will romp in with a red mouth and a gash under its left eye. It will race at her until she rushes into the Doctor's private office where she will find him x-raying fish. His hands will be raw from washing.

Francis Picabia

AHEAD AND BEHIND

I had a friend once, a Swiss fellow, Hans Bonkers by name. He
was living in Peru, twelve thousand feet up. He had gone there explor-
ing a few years before, and had lost his heart to the charms of a strange
Indian woman, who had driven him utterly out of his mind with love
unrequited. Little by little he had begun to waste away until, finally, he
was too weak even to leave his cabin. A Peruvian doctor who had
accompanied him on his travels treated him as best he could for a *de-
mentia praecox*, which he felt, however, to be quite incurable.

One night, a sudden influenza epidemic struck the little Indian vil-
lage where Hans Bonkers was being cared for. Every one of the na-
tives contracted the disease, without exception. In a few days, of the
original two hundred, one hundred seventy-eight were dead. In a panic,
the Peruvian doctor hurried back to Lima . . . My friend, stricken like all
the rest, lay languishing with fever.

Now, it happened that all of the Indians had one or more dogs, who
soon had no choice, if they were to survive, but to eat their dead mas-
ters. And so they proceeded to dismember their cadavers. One of them
came trotting into Hans Bonkers' hut, carrying in its mouth the head of
the Indian woman he adored . . . He recognized it at once. The shock,
I imagine, was so intense that it jarred him back to his senses, curing
him of both his fever and his madness. He took the head in his hands
and, with renewed vigor, playfully threw it across the room, telling the
dog to "go fetch!" Once, twice, three times . . . And the beast would
dutifully retrieve it, clutching it by the nose, in its teeth.

But the third time Hans Bonkers bowled a little too hard, and the
head smashed against the wall. As the brain rolled out he was delighted
to observe that it consisted of two smooth, rounded hemispheres, that
looked for all the world like a pair of firm buttocks . . .

From *Jésus-Christ Rastaquouère*
Translated from the French
by **Norman R. Shapiro**

Cristian Popescu

TRADITION

Ever since the No. 26 trolley began running, my family has reserved this very seat in this very car. Look at the little plaque with our family name. Here is where my father always sat, here is where my grandfather sat. They would sit motionless with a ticket in their hand, with a smile on their lips. Now it's my turn. Now I'm the one who maintains the collection of picture postcards of all the stops the 26 makes along its route. From my father I learned to paint the window every once in a while with clear nail polish to brighten the views.

When I decide to get off and see my wife, I place a manikin on my seat, a likeness of me, and I stick the ticket between its fingers. A manikin dressed in my wedding suit. And when I return, I find lipstick smeared on its cheeks from the young ladies who dare not kiss me in the flesh. Each night I bring my wife and children to the depot, I help them onto the car, and, perched on the driver's seat, I turn the crank and clang the trolley's bell on the hour until the first pale light of dawn.

Translated from the Romanian
by **Adam J. Sorkin** and
Bogden Ştefănescu

Constance Pultz

THE SPECTATOR

It's as if I'm always waiting for the next scene to happen, waiting for you or you or you to make a move. It's enough for me to watch the action taking place around me, knowing I needn't stir an inch to be a part of what's important. I was born being certain of things other people have to learn from books, studying the brush of the hand and the long gaze, memorizing footnotes that explain how some professor is scheduled to ask the student-actor if he is ready to take his place on the stage. For my part I whisper words that could be Yes or No or Perhaps, relying for my true answer on the movement of other people's lives, sure that in the course of time someone will make the gesture that will tilt my world in a new direction.

Jacques Réda

All sorts of rubbish is floating about in the canal underneath the moveable bridge, its machinery thick with grease and with hardly a cog on the wheels. The shape of a bottle can still be easily recognized, but the flabby dead forms brought alive by the plopping water turn the blood cold. And here is where you see it, less than a hundred metres past the rue de Crimée and its ancient barbarity, the living embodiment of the new barbarity. There it is, opposite warehouses with whole bushes projected from their brick-pillared corners, thrusting itself up in a single narrow block over more than thirty floors, white in the blue sky which is raging like a furious angel. Why would it not assume this appearance of a block of flats? So it does. Clouds go scurrying over its head in terror. And knowing nothing of angels or blocks of flats perhaps they divulge its name. Then something else happens on the same path they are following, across the Canal de l'Ourcq: a sort of slow-motion eruption of a mountain of smoke, as blue as a segment of the Juras, and we— a passing postman and myself—stare at each other in amazement at the exuberance of the world.

Translated from the French
by **Mark Treharne**

Jacques Réda

The fairground starts just after the wing of the building bearing the sign
Public Baths; it threads along the quayside, the shooting-galleries on
the right with rifles and bunches of feathers, and on the left a few
roundabouts, and not a cry coming from them. Arabs in their Sunday
best stand apart, meditating, and on the benches between the booths
retired couples are dozing. The fairground people themselves stand with
their backs to the deserted esplanade. In an aluminum fog over the
newly-built factories on the outskirts, in the gardens where people stand
looking at the smoke from heaps of grass scythed the day before, the
daylight goes on and on fading. There is so much space around the
place that it is better to stand still, or to go round in circles like the
tuneless wooden horses.

Translated from the French
by **Mark Treharne**

Pierre Reverdy

COMBAT AREA

On the empty chamber there is an aureole. The plants bordering the fringes of the roof down to the roots and even the blond leaves bring shadow.

The fourth wall goes further back. Further than the angle where the curtain is sighing. Higher than the pitch-black night and the shifting smoke from the factory. People are singing next to the empty chamber, against the roof, near the star.

There is an aureole which is not the moon, a brightness which is not a lamp. But a black square on the dark earth.

And this square, the empty chamber.

From *La balle au bond*
Translated from the French
by **Michel Delville**

Pierre Reverdy

BEHIND THE EYELIDS

Inside the tree—stars, images and electric wires sketching flashes of
lightning. In the center the characters are dancing on a cloud which
does not move. The hand of a sleeping child flutters around the lights—
without touching them. Kneeling before the hearth, he says a prayer.
And in the darkness where everybody is spinning round and round—in
blackness—the war goes on. In the city where the sunlight of old is
dying, the war goes on. The bed is rolling down the path leading to the
roof. And the head, smiling at the dream, full of chimes and plans of
glory, keeps going.

From *La balle au bond*
Translated from the French
by **Michel Delville**

Yannis Ritsos

EVENING WALK

Houses have their secrets. They signal back and forth by means of colors, carvings, windows, anthemions, chimneys in the most unlikely and suggestive postures. Stepping out my door, I catch them talking in whispers. They immediately fall silent, and their facades turn serious, as if a stranger had barged in on an intimate gathering. They wear the displeased expression of a man interrupted while drinking his tea, the hand holding the teacup arrested a little below chin-level. Just so the streets. No sooner do they see me coming than they hurriedly seal up their secrets, now under the traffic-lights at the corner, now under the few pepper trees, now in the shadow of a parked truck. They remind me of the huge buffet in the house I grew up in. It was always kept locked. Behind the fine cut glass, which reflected the bright squares of the windows in miniature, I could sense the delicate liqueur glasses, the little silver spoons that were brought out only for special guests, a giant fork for serving caviar, the porcelain, the jars full of candied oranges, and something else, I don't remember, they never let me see it, on the top shelf, I was so small I couldn't reach that high, not even the time I pulled over a chair and climbed up, one afternoon when mother was out and they'd left the buffet unlocked. "Good evening, Ariosto, how are you?" I hear an oddly gentle voice. It's a colleague from the office. His voice feels sorry for me. I can see in his eyes how sad and unshaven I look. The sunset flashes on balcony railings and in windows, at once lugubrious and magnificent. And I am like a man whose wife left him the day before, and he walks the street knowing that his house is locked, that its rooms are empty, that a fine layer of dust is forming along the backs of the furniture, and all that's left, on the arm of the sofa, are her worn, tan gloves, which she forgot at the last moment. Yet the evening spills over with colors—yellow, pink, cobalt, deep purple, and a gold chalice filled with warm water. I dip my fingers in the water. I wipe them on a piece of white cloth. I raise the chalice. Now I can hold services all alone in the world.

Translated from the Greek
by **Martin McKinsey**

Vern Rutsala

HANNELORE

All through your childhood she was like a rumor, a few hints caught in the aftermath of hushed talk, your mother suddenly busy at the sink, your father unduly curious about your school day. Remember how she turned up in only a couple of faded pictures in the album—a vague face in the background, sketchy features scarcely evident in the dim sepia. And though you have no direct memory of her presence your sense of her persists, a long skirt swirling out of the nineteenth century, a darkness, a sense of loss, a casualty.

Remember that car trip that went on longer than the usual outings. You knew it was serious because your father wore his suit—he kept tugging with his fingers inside the collar of his starched shirt. There was a hushed sadness inside the car, your mother speaking softly and your father driving without telling his usual jokes or commenting on the merits of the farmland you passed.

He stopped the car in a gravel parking lot in front of a large brick building. It looked cold and the windows seemed vacant as blind eyes. You knew she was there. Only your father went in. You and your mother walked around the small town and stopped for ice cream in a little drug store. When you got back to the car your father wasn't there and then he showed up walking slowly and looking down, scuffing his good shoes through the gravel. After he got in the car it shocked you when he started crying. You had never seen him cry. "She's just not there," he said several times as your mother stroked his shoulder. Then he blew his nose and drove off. All the way home the feeling in the car had the fuzzy sadness of Sunday nights when school loomed the next day and the frail freedom of the weekend was lost. Only it was worse than that.

Later, you learned she had waited in Germany for seven years for her husband to make enough money for her to join him in America. Working in copper mines and on roadgangs, he eventually felt able to take a homestead and sent her the passage money. You have thought of her days of waiting—the teasing from her brother, the gossip in the town—and what her journey to this country must have been. We can't conceive such distances and hardships, complaining as we do when a plane is an hour late or the flight attendant runs out of those little packages of honey-almonds. A small woman in her twenties, she came by sea and over land without knowing the language, unsure of where she was going. She never deigned to learn proper English, which suggests the kind of half-world she lived in. The harsh winters, the childbirth, the fretting loneliness, watching her children become increasingly alien as they went to school and came back speaking words she couldn't understand, making fun of her old-fashioned ways.

Not long after you got married your mother told you about her wedding night. There was no money for anything like a honeymoon so the newlyweds were at the old farm and had gone to bed when Hannelore came struggling into their room with a folding cot and insisted on spending the night.

You remember dim bits of the farm—the house looming like a barn with cold-smelling rooms, rough floors, the attic where you found a broken cast-iron bank in the shape of a train. There was the thick light and heavy odor of the real barn, too, and the threat of the irrigation ditch you had to drive over and the wide blond fields. You have glimpses of these but not of her. The Depression took the farm. Something darker took her.

John Shoemaker

YOUR TIME WILL COME

Aunt Mary is coming! Aunt Mary, who gave you a bow tie on your birthday and a children's bible for Christmas. And look, it's Uncle Dave too! How he loves to hold you on his lumpy lap, snorting and laughing, his breath a fine mist from drinks that only grownups are allowed. No use trying to escape. It makes him too happy when you wiggle and squirm. At least he buys you presents you really want. And loves you best of all, since you know how to keep a secret. Still, you're not quite happy. What is it that's wrong with you? Is something missing? If only your mother would let you have that puppy. You could take it deep into the woods behind your house and beat it with a belt.

Barry Silesky

SAVED

Like that dream where she really wanted you—gleam of skin, breast, cock—The usual compensations? Then trash on waking, mixed with the swollen leg, throbbing while someone tore up the back door in the night, and the house was stripped. All over the world the shooting goes on. Then the doorbell rings and the pain is actually gone. With the notes buried in the counter's daily junk pile, you had no idea you'd even entered. Now it's another city. No paradise, but all the blood, sex, he, she, flushed away. It's not all luck. You have to pay attention, send in the entry. Now, I can quit this stupid job, take over the building, gifts to all our friends. We can be lost again, actual ghosts wandering the streets. All we've got to do is keep out of sight. Of course that's impossible. It's time to clean the gun.

Barry Silesky

HOLY DAY

And things were going so well—you winning the drawing, me getting the raise as our team soars to the top, the screaming almost gone. Ok, so I hit the kid again, he deserved it. Pain, tears, ice to the spot, but no bruise anyone could see. He's got to learn. Besides, he's fine now; I'm the one sick with it. Isn't this sadness enough? It could be an echo of the famous trial, wife beaten and murdered with her boyfriend, the killer set free. He's so sorry. We think it helped him to be famous. But the rest of us? The doctor injects the serum, we get tired, immunity breaks down, we're overcome. Cancel my subscription, turn off that popular song.

AvenuMalkenu: for the sin that I have sinned against thee: a day fasting, hope for another year, and better—don't you understand? Luckily, we've stopped expecting that.

Charles Simic

THESEUS AND ARIADNE

I shall go about with my eyes closed. The streets will no longer be safe. False Messiah, I'm going to step on your tin cup and tambourine. I'll brush against missing children, a few murderers and their sweethearts. Someone with onions on his breath will put a gold watch against my ear. It'll be like silent laughter. I'll be spun around by the crowd like a carousel.

I hope she'll still follow me. I'll cross bridges. I'll reach Jersey meadows if I have to. "He's a lost seeing-eye dog," she'll say. "In the blind universe he wants to be blind like love." O she won't even be there! Up and down Broadway where I play my game.

Charles Simic

EUPHEMIA GRAY'S PUBIS

For John Yau

As for me, I like them with plenty of hair, Mr. Ruskin. I remember soaping the crotch of a certain Miss L. in the sea at dusk, while she soaped mine. The water was cold, but we were burning. Our kisses made the night hurry, the sun take its time setting.

Marble nymphs in the park surrounded by purse snatchers, how sad they always seem! Lay down your bow and arrows, Daphne, and grill us some sausages on the stove. Your ass is bare, your hair is in wild disarray. The sound of our antique bedsprings reaches to the museum across the street.

The visitors don't know what to make of it. Someone is moaning, someone is whispering obscenities around the child Madonna. They pretend not to hear, they stop to view and admire her briefly, and then stroll on, like fish in a fishtank we'll be having for late dinner tonight.

Charles Simic

HEROIC MOMENT

I went bare-assed into the battle. The President himself heard of my insolence. I was given a flea-ridden mutt to ride. I rode in company of crows pleading with them to please remember me. I had a dollhouse knife between my teeth, the red plastic pisspot on my head as a helmet.

When she heard the news, my mother caused the Greek fleet to be deprived of favorable winds on its way to Troy. Witch, they called her, dirty witch—and she, so pretty, chopping the onions, laughing and crying over the stew pot.

Charles Simic

VOICE FROM THE CAGE

Mr. Zoo Keeper, will you be making your rounds today? We are howling, we are clucking in distress. It's been ages since you've come. We smell awful, we smell to high heaven. Sorrow, sickness, and flea bites are our lot.

The rabbits still screw but their weakness is optimism. Even the lion doesn't believe the fables any more. "Pray to the Lord," the monkeys shriek. I've dyed my hair green like Baudelaire. The big circus tent, I tell everybody, still stands in the distance. I can see the trumpets glow. I can hear the snare drum.

Ours is a circus of quick, terrified glances.

Goran Simić

MEDALS

When he returned from the war my grandfather locked himself up in the attic and did not come out for fifteen days. During the day he was silent and at night he would moan so terribly that the candles under the icon would go out. My grandmother saw the faces of death when he finally came down.

When my father returned from the war in his bloodstained overcoat, he spilled a heap of medals from his bag and went up to the attic without looking at anyone. During the day we would compare his medals with grandfather's, and at night we would put our heads under the pillows so as not to hear him calling his dead friends and moaning. Come morning, my mother would place his shiny medals on the window for passers-by to see. But no one passed by our house anymore because no one could stand the moaning. One morning we found a ghost in the overcoat by the bed. The ghost watching with his own eyes.

It happened a long time ago. The family vault has thickened. The medals still hang on the walls, and sometimes the clerks take them during the holidays and return them after a couple of days. I would not even notice if they never returned them. Only sometimes, after I'm horrified by the news of the war, I see them on the wall. Because the only thing left from my father and grandfather are the screams and moans, and I console myself that it is the wind scratching the damaged attic beams of our simple house.

Translated from the Bosnian
by **Amela Simić**
and **Christopher Merrill**

Goran Simić

WAR MICE

In the second summer of war the town was swamped with mice. At night rats would come out of the sewer and occupy the empire of the trash dump. They would sometimes attack naive cats and lost children, and with the first dark we would lock our doors. As if by secret agreement, our apartments were inhabited by small, stupid mice we would discover in our flour supplies and among Sunday clothes, and the more we exterminated them, the more there were. The first one caught in the mousetrap behind the piano we named "the artist," and later followed a nameless army of mice that only had numbers.

I thought: even I remember only the name of the first victim who died for this town, and then came the black statistics of dead Sarajevans. What was her name? I try to remember and I bring from the attic a box of obituary notices. But I find inside only scraps of paper and the frightened eyes of the mice-nation we have not managed to destroy for centuries, though they do not even know the name of their first victim. Nor the name of their homeland they left long ago.

Translated from the Bosnian
by **Amela Simić**
and **Christopher Merrill**

William Slaughter

CHINA LESSON

What's he thinking, I'm thinking, the real live Panda Bear? As he rides his motor-bike around the ring in the Shanghai Acrobatic Theater where he's a featured performer. With a look, an air, of complacency about him. He's thinking private thoughts. More than his trainer knows, who turns in the center of the ring pointing approvingly at the Panda Bear. The trainer is completely taken in. He believes the applause is for him. But the Panda Bear is nobody's fool. He has an above average IQ and a diploma from Panda Bear School. He has learned his China lesson well. His eyes, and the expression on his face, reveal nothing. Give nothing away. He's keeping it all in, saving it for himself. The Panda Bear has a secret. One night—tonight?—he's going to break the circle with his trainer still pointing approvingly at him and ride his motorbike out of the theater into the night. He knows exactly what he's doing. Who can stop him? The Panda Bear has done his homework. Has studied geography. The map of China is in his head as he rides south out of Shanghai toward the border crossing at Shenzhen. Panda Bears don't need passports to get into the New Territories and Hong Kong. They just go. He'll take up residence there in a small flat—in Stanley, say— and live a quiet life anonymously. Perhaps he'll have a stall on the waterfront where he'll sell small replicas of himself which he'll draw with brush and ink using his own right paw. Doing a tidy business. Smiling all the while. Never looking back.

Bruce Smith

AMERIKA

The K we wrote into America was like prying apart the jaws of the 60s and inserting our heads. The teeth were the 50s—white, enameled like the fridge. Hanoi was where we were headed, headless as we were, and fuck Dad eking out his dying. We took the K from him, Republican golfer that he was, like Ike and his klan. It was too late to go to Selma or San Francisco, to be clubbed and dogbitten and loved. Writing it had the dizzying thrill of self-strangulation or sin. We were never sure if he heard, upstairs, but fuck him on general principles. Each accommodating consonant we'd make awkward, hammering the Ks of the folding chairs with our fists. Apparently he never heard the manifestos and position papers. Softly, safely, we let the drugs come over us. We took the K from neocolonial khaki, Yankee, kike, stroke, bunko artist, the Judas kiss.

Ellen McGrath Smith

A PARISIAN DINNER

Almost overnight, an agreement has been made between me and the man from Perigord. He is not to flirt with me. He is not to take a seat beside me in the resto-U without inquiring now, first with his eyes. He is no longer allowed to pretend he is, like the others here, a student with a future. Even with his briefcase full of soiled papers, even with his papers full of countless figures, he is not permitted to pretend he is someone to contend for me; he is old and bald and needs a bath; I couldn't eat; I was ready to gag; he had gone through the wastecans to make up his plate. I stood up as he came to sit down. "You're not going to throw that out, are you?" he asked me furtively, the way he used to ask before: "Would you like to spend a weekend in Perigord with me?"

Thomas R. Smith

WINDY DAY AT KABEKONA

Only a picture window stands between us and the full force of gusts that lift the branches of the red pine. Draft under the cabin door rolls the rug resolutely into a tube despite our attempts to lay it flat.

Foot-high waves spume across the lake; near shore the color of the long, gleaming swells softens to a milky jade, warmer looking than it is, almost southern. But the drift of this world is northerly; lawn chairs are hurled into woodpiles, propellers of outboard motors scrape against stones. The door bangs loosely in its sill. Jack pines groan as if they could snap and fall.

There is something in all this fury that makes the day oceanic: We're near at any moment being swamped, drowned, pinned by wreckage. In the cloudless sky, the sun gleefully conducts the turbulence as though it were Wagnerian opera. A gull white as our idea of angels hovers above the shore for a moment—fully awake—fighting the wind before being torn from its place.

Linda Smukler

RADIO

She sits with her legs stretched out on top of the radio fan blowing up
between   a baby reaches up and out the bars are high its face is red it
cries "a something ma—ma—a something ma" over and over the fan
muffles the sound but it's there in the room like a spreading rash the
weather's too hot for anything let alone a baby too hot to hear it and
smell its puke and no one around to help but the baby's grandfather and
the girls downstairs   too hot to get up and turn off the Andrews Sisters
her husband's off working and it's a shame   thought he'd make more
of himself than building houses and coming home smelling like tar and
sawdust it's a dirty business and on top of it all they have to live here
paint chipping off the ceiling and walls falling down   no other way to
afford a place and her own father on the ground floor running his bar
or more like he just watches it run no way this child's gonna grow up
around drunks and freaks and its grandfather slinking around haunting
its heart the baby's cries get louder lost three before this one shut up
blow on it soap it down she gets up and picks up the fan she points
it directly on the baby walks into the kitchen and comes back carrying
a blue tray of ice turns the ice tray over and stands there as the icecubes
bounce off the baby's head ice little baby feel good? that's real fine
she walks out of the room and slams the door the fan drowns out the
baby's screams ice melting around its ears

Linda Smukler

PRAYER

(I started to write & the letter upset me & I called and cried & you washed the sheets & had me pray.)

So you said and yes I like lipstick not on me on you you cried on the phone overwhelmed by my love and yours by all the too many words by your days which go by now too fast with too much work and not enough time by your cold by and for desire you cried in your home sitting in your blue plaid chair next to the low table low chair and the couch we made love on which now holds your lover passed out on dark wine you cried and asked if I was sleeping upstairs tonight you cried because I said no because I said I washed the sheets and tried to tell you why: I woke this morning upstairs in the guest room where you slept with me which is my room really as it holds my books my rain man kachina my volcano my fertility my rocks I slept there the night before (Monday) and the night before that (Sunday) which was the day you drove off into the dark I slept there because I did not want to lose you but I woke hot and dry from the woodstove I woke wanting to forget you were far away again to forget that when I went to sleep I held you in my mind and felt you hold me but also felt the shadow of your lover next to you I woke thinking it was time to sleep in a cooler place time to sleep in the bed downstairs where I had slept for five years with my lover to sleep on the side of the bed I chose near the window for quick escape and to look out at the weather (the only windows upstairs I needed and had were your mouth and the fragrant dawn of your hair) I woke and intended to sleep downstairs my back turned to the wide expanse of the bed to wake up and to look out at my pine tree and the empty bird feeder and everything that was safe and everything that kept me separate and alone

The night you called and cried I did sleep downstairs but before I slept I also prayed and I prayed again when I got up and like you I rose in the dawn freed and in love and in the new morning you said (on the phone again) Look but don't touch and for the first time claimed me for your own

Maura Stanton

SEARCHES

Once again TV detectives are searching the suspects' rooms in some old rambling house in England. The Chief Inspector opens the bureau drawers in tiers, pulling out striped ties and folded white shirts; he sniffs every cut-glass bottle; he ruffles through papers on the desk, unclasps a small leather book and turns unerringly to the suspicious entry. In another room his tweed-coated assistant pushes back filmy dresses, and holds up a black high heel, checking for traces of a red garden clay. "Why is there a dead wasp on the nightstand?" he wonders aloud, while his superior calls him across the hall. "Why has someone thrown a glass of brandy into the freplace?" Red herrings, these questions will never be answered, but the two men exchange knowing looks as the musical score, something in imitation of Elgar, swells in excitement. Downstairs in a library of mullioned windows and walls of gilt-stamped books, the impatient suspects drink sherry and smoke cigarettes, their faces twitching, their eyes shifty or worried or insouciant. Later, alone here in my own room, I wonder if I have any secrets from myself, and I open my top drawer briskly to see who this person is who calls herself by my name. What's this? All these curious hair ornaments, barrettes, tortoise shell combs, silvery elastic bands. Here's a snood; here are chiffon ribbons and satin ribbons; a box full of black bobby pins with blunt plastic tips and another containing thin sharp spidery hairpins; here's an ancient torn hairnet for blonds; here's an unopened package containing a nylon flexible comb tossed on top of jeweled pony-tail holders, a lime-plastic device for creating a French roll, a spongy nylon doughnut for a bun, and more barrettes, some cloisonné, others burnished metal. Oh how unerringly a detective's hands sort through this distracting clutter! The camera zooms in on a small box of "Bronchial-Pastillen" from the Hertenstein Drogerie in Lucerne, Switzerland. Throat lozenges or cyanide tablets? I'm as surprised as the audience when I pry open the tin lid to discover a catch of fifty yellowed slips saved from the centers of crisp fortune cookies devoured years ago in forgotten Chinese restaurants. What can it mean? The camera moves in on my expression. Another red herring? Or the real clue to her existence?

J. David Stevens

THE SIGN

Wishing immortality, he built a sign bearing his name in the mountains of Montana. The sign stood over thirty feet tall, on four steel pylons sunk into concrete beds. The name itself was made from small pieces of colored glass which he spent several months soldering carefully into place.

His hopes for the sign were great. After he died, he imagined, an unsuspecting hunter would stumble across the sign and throw the switch that ignited the several rows of alternating, multi-colored lights. Stunned by its beauty, the hunter would report back to people in town, who would spread the word to family and friends. Soon the sign would become a tourist spot. New roads would lead to its feet—or, far into the future, people would approach by hovercraft and wonder at the name emblazoned in crystal and light. Stories would circulate. The sign would become myth. And after the first representatives of the Zarnax Empire landed on Earth, they would carry across the galaxy stories of a learned people who had seen the name of their god written in the hills and thus been saved.

But things didn't work out quite that way. After his death, the few hunters who happened by took pot shots at the sign, destroying whole sections of the intricately arranged glass. A new freeway drew travelers to the south, making area roads obsolete. And even the Zarnaxians never landed, deciding that Earth was worth neither friendship nor conquest.

Not that the sign went completely forgotten. Every now and then, on a crisp autumn night, a teenage boy would take his date into the hills to see the sign that his drunken uncle had once recalled on a hunting trip. He would throw the switch, and the rows of light would shine like a beacon, reflecting off the piecemeal shards of glass. There the boy and girl would share their first kiss, or something else. And eventually they would marry and move east to cities like Grand Forks or St. Paul, west to Boise or Seattle.

And years later, when people would ask how they came to choose one another, he would recall a drunken uncle who told legends about signs in the hills. And she would remember mesmerizing rows of splendid light, spreading beyond the mountains, beyond all spans of time and distance. The light, they agreed, symbolized their love—a jagged ember lodged intractably in their hearts, a surrender written in color for all eternity.

Brian Swann

THE DIRECTOR

In delightful settings, he developed the tenuous connections between cosmic and comic for the mass market. Then one day he stumbled upon her, Dolly, nude, trying to pry the gold leaf off the abandoned set of a flamboyant decade. His work suffered, but all went well until one night when Tina, his wife of thirty years, woke to find him floating sumptuously in sleep, another name on his lips, his night clothes knotted. She intended to be epic with repercussions this time, so through mostly legal methods she hastened his entrapment. Then left. This raised possibilities in his mind. To think about them he would spend whole mornings watching gray fog cover the lotus flowers on the lake. He wondered if the rape of a clown would provide focus, but gave it up as too poetic, noting, however, how the literal can be touched with new dimensions, like the white walls of a boarding house in late summer. From there, the impulse was away from what he knew—tormented marriages, mistresses with criminal tendencies (the clay of comic drama)—to pure conjecture, "things that prove nothing" (Truffaut). So, caught up, he sought to capture, without capturing, the glance, say, of someone who seemed without illusions. As he walked along the lake, by now empty of flowers, empty of all save sky, he practiced his mock signature in air, all form, no substance, like a German industrialist he once knew with his own postwar horror. His ex told the press he was planning to film a doorman's life because he has none. But she had her own agenda, and it could be said that he was on the way to having none.

Jean Tardieu

MAN AND HIS SHADOW

The defeat of idols has not stifled in us the desire to construct some huge creature, alien to reason, capable of containing all of our anxieties and, at the same time, conduct us to the doors of an incorruptible empire, adorned with the august prestige of impersonality.

Yet, by a bizarre paradox, since nothing, even that which lies on the edge of emptiness, can tear us away from the memory of our condition, it would seem that the first of these mythic figures, still obscure and quivering, like a newborn world, is man himself.

In the definitions that he gives to his own nature, to his destiny, there is not a trait, not a notion that does not surpass him. His gigantic shadow drags him along and he follows it, moaning.

From *La part de l'ombre*
Translated from the French
by **James Vladimir Gill**

James Tate

DENIED AREAS

Some zones you have to walk around. We have no idea what goes on inside them, we just give them a wide berth and look around for the friendlier zones. Sometimes you have to take running leaps to get to them. We keep moving, not always in straight lines, but we keep moving. And we can chat, "How's the weather?" "I don't know." "How's your mother?" "I don't have a mother." It can be stressful, though sometimes we break into song without warning, and then someone always starts to remember another life, and then one by one we all begin to weep and anything seems possible, like a glistening rainy pavement, or a lodging house, a toothpick.

James Tate

TO EACH HIS OWN

When Joey returned from the war he worked on his motorcycle in the garage most days. A few of his old buddies were still around— Bobby and Scooter—and once or twice a week they'd go down to the club and have a few beers. But Joey never talked about the war. He had a tattoo on his right hand that said DEVI and he wouldn't even tell what that meant. Months passed and Joey showed no interest in getting a job. His old Indian motorcycle ran like a top, it gleamed, it purred. One night at dinner he shocked us all by saying, "Devi's coming to live with us. It's going to be difficult. She's an elephant."

James Tate

ALL OVER THE LOT

    We were at the ballgame when a small child came up to me and thwacked me in my private area. He turned and walked away without a single word. I was in horrible pain for a couple of minutes, then I went looking for the rascal. When I found him he was holding his mother's hand and looking like the picture of innocence. "Is that your son?" I asked of the lady. She shot me a look that could fry eggs, and then she slapped me really hard. "Mind your own business," she screaked. The boy grinned up at me. My old tweed vest was infested with fleas. I started walking backwards. People were shoving me this way and that. To each I replied, "God, I love this game, I love this game."

James Tate

HER SILHOUETTE AGAINST THE ALPENGLOW

Climbing a mountain is very hard work so we just sat at the bottom of it and ate our picnic. Others came along and actually started to climb it. They were tough and strong but we still thought they were foolish, but refrained from telling them so. They were loaded down with so much equipment they could barely walk on level ground—ropes, sleeping bags, tents, hammers, pitons, lamps, food supplies, ice axes, oxygen masks—whereas for a picnic you can get everything you need into a basket—wine, cheese, salami, bread, napkins. "Marie," I said, "Do you still love me?" "Chuck you, Farley," she said, "and your whole famn damily. You know I'll always love you. All's hotsie-dandy here, thank you very much."

Carine Topal

MAX IN EGYPT

Years ago, years ago, my mother and her mother left Dresden, city of gold-rimmed porcelain and fine china cups, to take the train to another country, dip into the mud and mineral baths at Trencin Teplice. It was Czechoslovakia, 1933. There they would crouch and turn until the wet earth shrunk from the early sun and became their second skin.

Grandpa Max sailed to Egypt where he schooled dark-haired Fatimas in the art of western romance. He called all the girls Yasmine. It was the *khamsin*, time of the hot winds which left men, like grandpa, sipping mint tea, sucking the *nahna* until there was nothing but a withered mint leaf on his marble-white left hand, because in his right, he held his cigarette, German style, index finger pointing, tapping ashes of the cigarettes he lit and handed out lavishly to young girls, girls from the province of Sawhaj, girls from towns with names that sang Zagzig, Akhim, Ismailia.

The tips of grandpa's index and mid-finger were saffron-yellow. And he pressed these fingers to take the pinky of one girl, any one, and he pressed these fingers to take the nipple of another and twist it in his mouth, then watch it return, glimmering from saliva. And the nipples, when dried and pink, had a yellow tinge too.

Grandpa Max lived an extraordinary life, drawn into the circle of glittering objects, snake charmers and transvestite dancers. The pleasure of female pursuit was here, in Cairo and Alexandria. Here, the smells of the souk—zatar and sesame—the endless carpets and billowing trousers floating from the walls. A boat ride down the Nile. Who would have known that in several years, Max's life would be a ship filled with Persian carpets, crystal chandeliers and all that fleeing Jews could carry.

Helen Tzagoloff

MAIL-ORDER BRIDE

He had many responsibilities—dinners with elderly mother, tennis on Saturdays. Didn't she want him to be fit? Drinks with the boss, that's how it is in America, if you want to advance.

At breakfast he read the newspaper. In the evening they watched snatches of shows on television. "Such junk," he declared, switching channels. She longed for conversation and tea with fragrant, old-world bread. "I'd like to have a baby," she told him. "Let's wait. Maybe I'm too old. This is such a nice life," he said.

When she became a citizen, she moved to a one-room basement apartment, found a job in a nursing home. Some said she was selfish and calculating.

Mark Vinz

LETTER FROM THE CABIN

for Jay and Martha

I've watched all week, but it seems the eagles really haven't returned this year. The heron's nest on the other side of the inlet is deserted, too, though high water and tricky winds make it impossible to get out in the boat most days. Still, it's enough to look up from whatever page I'm turning and watch the lake—the long trajectory of loons skimming the water, wings beating waves, echoing cries. You know how they always thrill us, especially at night.

It's humid today, the thick clouds seeming to grow from the shore—when friends are here, it's what we scarcely notice, up late, talking quietly on the screened-in porch. In the morning there is always time to take turns stretching out on the dock, to be alone with birds and sky and water. And now, as dinner wine is cooling in the refrigerator, you're here again, all of us peering out into the fading light, amazed by wind in leaves, full of smiles for this other life—the one where we're totally thankful.

Mark Vinz

THE GETAWAY

He's been like this for days, ever since we got here—just sitting there in front of the porch screen staring at the lake, watching the shifting wind ripple the water, the sunlight on the leaves. He waves to every passing boat, every bird. "Loon," he cries. "Crow, mallard, great blue heron!" To tell the truth, we're starting to get worried. "I'm going to order some binoculars," he calls out, "and a canoe just like that one. I wonder if it comes in green."

We even have to bring him dinner on a tray, out there in the fading light where he's cheering the squirrels and chipmunks. And now, when it's too dark to see anymore, he's made a bed out of blankets and pillows. We can hear him most of the night—flat on his back, dozing, watching above his toes. "Firefly," he shouts. "Shooting star!"

Chris Volpe

NOT 'WHY BUILD' BUT 'WHICH TOOLS'

The neighborhood is buzzing with the news: someone's going to be resurrected like Lazarus at midnight.

A distant cousin writes of plans to set himself on fire and enter his hometown post office. Something about a letter he could never bring himself to send. I once owned a letter-opener in the shape of a tiny silver sword. I used it to rid an undiscovered country of villains and dangerous beasts. Last night our garage was dragged off, piece by piece, and buried somewhere by the neighbor's dog. It was blue with pink tasseled window shades. No sense rushing things, but somebody's got to feed that dog.

If you get out of bed just right, says Thoreau, anything at all is possible. The universe is tall as a runway. At dawn, white and silver ironing boards and irons drift lazily across an orange-pink sky.

Diane Wald

WHAT PERHAPS YOU DON'T UNDERSTAND

If I wanted music I would say so. I will not answer the phone. I don't care how I seem to the electric meter reader. I don't want to eat any dinner. I am honored to make these decisions. I don't have to like these movies. You can ask me to go with you, but you cannot demand that I like it. I don't want you looking over my shoulder. I don't want you reading over my shoulder. Today I don't even want you to look at my shoulder. This is the law. That is the way it is. Myrtle is the name of a flower. Thank you.

Liz Waldner

POST PRANDIAL

for SweetBee Smoothfield

Time, fine, a fine time was had by all. The tine of the fork, the fork of the tree, the tree of life, the life of Reilly and now it's either Irish or smiley. Eyes, nays, *pince nez,* sweat bee. A sweat bee reconnoitering me. The cicada sound swells and dies like the sea on the sand, like the breeze in the trees. The bee's still reconnoitering me. An orange-edged winged thing flies by fast. The band about my brain tightens. The buzz saw, the band saw, song of some bug, and the sweat bee lands on my blue muu-muu, probes to be sure it's missing nothing sweet. Its eyes attuned to another frequency, it can't be sure. Me, neither. SweetBee, hello. I am fickle. Something stung me at yesterday evening's dinner party. It left a welt like missing you.

Rosmarie Waldrop

THIS

When the medulla oblongata is pricked, or in any other way irritated, the white furious sun high in a state of tension. Shed her clothes and inexplicably married. Caught in the fact. The first representations of Amerindians showed naked men and women gnawing on a human leg with equal opportunity. Her husband avoided looking directly into her face.

While nervous power is necessary to muscular motion the sun cannot be replaced by logic. Hence the inhabitants of New England have never made friends without blinds drawn. Solitary muscles, such as the sphincter, are always contracted. The Indians stood between quotation marks. While an oblique ray of sunlight penetrates a silk blouse the stimulus is shown as consistent. In all his life, he had seen nothing that so delighted his parts.

Likewise, a quick thrust on the toe-pad excites language and a shade too sure of herself. Subcutaneous itch. To fight it out in whispers, in degrees Fahrenheit. Desire flaked off the shoulder of the highway, by way of blaming the sun. To introduce difference into the all-or-nothing theory, the women wore no covering other than a narrow cloth over their privates. A heavy penetrating odor caught on the person of her husband.

The sun's influence on nerves, though in small quantities, the angle of incidence sealing cooperation and paraphrase. As nature intended, there was hair on the rest of his body. In the upper half of the picture, the condition of sight itself. The longer the Indians stood in the sun, the more it turned their eyes back into their body. This was before she knew she was pregnant.

Charles Harper Webb

POMADES

The Chairman of a university Physics department develops "quite
a thing" for pomades.

He doesn't mention it to anyone. Not even in bed to his pretty
blonde wife twelve years his junior. Not even in his backyard, playing
badminton with his good-looking kids, a girl and a boy, ten and twelve
years old respectively, who do well in school, have lots of nice friends,
and are perfectly adjusted.

He denies the "thing" to himself. He denies even the need to deny
having denied it. He in no way ever, not for one split second, indicates
the presence of the "thing." It's just as if the "thing" does not exist.

Except it does.

In the lecture hall; in the laboratory; at the beach playing frisbee; at
the symphony hearing Beethoven brutalized; at the laundromat wash-
ing his hunting pants and his wife's panties the day their washer broke;
at the podium chairing the biggest convention of internationally-renowned
physicists ever; relaxing in his chaise longue on his fresh-cut lawn on
summer evenings, watching pretty girls bounce by in tans and shorts
and halter-tops—loving his wife, and reflecting that life has been good
to him.

Pomades.

Oh sweet Jesus, pomades.

Charles Harper Webb

A STOCKBROKER DREAMS A STORY,

and tells it to three friends.

The world looks better to them instantly. Giggling like kindergartners, each skips away "to change my life."

"This must be a *peak experience*," the broker thinks. "The 90% of the brain people don't use, just worked for me!"

He sits to write his story down, but can't remember all of it. There were Clydesdales and albinos, he's sure, and action verbs—*escalate* and *vault* and *terrorize* and *decompose*—as well as nouns like *brethren, cistern, Boraxo, grandmother, cement mixer*. And the phrase *Telegram for Mr. Nosehair*—how did that fit in?

He calls his three friends. One has made a million in the stock market that hour. One has just married a beautiful heiress "with the kindest heart in the world." One has fulfilled his lifelong dream to be a "narchaeologist."

Each recalls a few words—*callipygian, hump, pseudo-encephalitis, string-saver, philodendrons in spring breeze*. These just confuse him more.

The story shifts, distorting as he gropes for it, like a cellophane bag floating in the sea.

He plays a relaxation tape, "Machu Pichu," hoping to fall back into the dream. Instead he dreams he's trying to dig sapphires out of concrete with a plastic spoon.

He wakes from that dream to find his story more faded than before. This is what happened to Coleridge, writing "Kubla Khan." Some farmer knocked, demanding payment for a cheese, and cut the poem off at the hip.

"Damn it," he howls, kicks a chair, and wakes up in his bed.

"What's wrong?" his wife mumbles. "You kicked me. . . ."

He tells about his dreams, including as much of the story as he can. After breakfast, he starts to write everything down. But it's like trying to grasp smoke.

His wife remembers he said *catalepsy, cataracts, catamaran*, and either *annihilate*, or *prevaricate*—"something with *ate* in it."

Staring at his empty page, he grinds his teeth, and feels himself waking from another dream.

"Oh no," he thinks. "Not the dream within a dream within a dream. Not waking and waking and waking. . . ."

His story—the masterpiece that could redeem his life—keeps dwindling: a snowball in the sun . . . a birthmark under skin creme . . . traces of a pimple, smaller every day . . . a planet knocked from orbit, moving off in a black sky . . .

Tom Whalen

BASEBALL

The games we played as children! The way the birds screeched at sunset and the earth swallowed the sun! Then Timmy would begin to cry and Billy would comfort him by whispering into his ear the names of forgotten shortstops and we would hide in the tall grass of the outfield with our gloves over our mouths. Always our summer days would end this way with the playing field scarred and our bats in splinters and our heads longing for the stars that soon would appear and form the constellation of Mother calling us inside. But we, with our warm breath and bones, did not want to return to our homes, we wanted to play on and on until the baseball broke apart like a dandelion, and the leaves fell, and the snows fell, and the air . . .

Tom Whalen

THE NEXT MORNING

"I'm going to pieces," Rodin said one sunny morning getting out of bed. "I've been bitten by minuscule monsters. And the giant eye that swirls in the fluid, what of *it*?"

The silence descended and he began to chew softly the air above his head until he made a space large enough to slip his body into. Which is how I found him when I came in.

"What are you doing without your spacesuit?" I asked.

M. L. Williams

CONNEMARA

The moment is singular. The bus falls through the landscape in the distance and nothing closes in. That is, it is a happy moment I share with a lover, but the lover doesn't enter against the light shattering over the green and silver land like fire. Everywhere is green and the ruins of an old cottage in the middle of it. There should be leprechauns lined against the black stone, but they have given up their stations long ago to become the bearded nuns of Limerick, whom I love absolutely. The bog gives a little under our feet; we walk on water. In this happiness resides what renders us completely alone. You turn, and I look back at the cold steel spine of the bus that refuses to dissolve even against desire, even against the prayer I say to keep it all inside me like the myth of anything's creation. The lyre in my hand means I never looked for you, Eurydice, I never looked back. When you check later, the ticket stub tells you everything your thumb has rubbed off, including the price of the journey.

Peter Wortsman

THE RIDDLE OF THE SPHINX

Sometimes, sound asleep, she lets out cries, foetal and almost unutterable, rousing you into sudden listening. The riddle of the sphinx must have been posed like this—howled—moaned—wept. You listen intently for an instant, try to decipher the unconsolable hieroglyphs, then embrace her without thinking. Shadow of a bird of prey passing, the unnamed sadness dissolves—in silence—or sometimes is repeated in the deafening howl of a delivery truck stalled in early morning traffic.

Peter Wortsman

GERTRUDE AND ALICE POSE

That, my dear Alice, is a device employed by the lazy voyeur to entrap his prey, Gertrude warns loud enough to be overheard by the man behind the camera. It reminds me of a Cyclops, Alice shudders. Precisely, Alice dear, says Gertrude gripping the arms of her easy chair, which is why we'd best be inconspicuous.—Will you have a cup of tea, Mr. Man Ray? The photographer declines. Gertrude concentrates hard, determined to become the chair. How dearly the walls love Alice, who easily melds with mildew and art. Gertrude is jealous at such natural facility, but too proud to show it. Sit up straight, she admonishes her companion, posterity has no patience for bad posture.

C.D. Wright

SONG OF THE GOURD

In gardening I continued to sit on my side of the car: to drive
whenever possible at the usual level of distraction: in gardening
I shat nails glass contaminated dirt and threw up on the new shoots:
in gardening I learned to praise things I had dreaded: I pushed the
hair out of my face: I felt less responsible for one man's death
one woman's longterm isolation: my bones softened: in gardening I lost
nickels and ring settings I uncovered buttons and marbles: I lay
half the worm aside and sought the rest: I sought myself in the bucket
and wondered why I came into being in the first place: in gardening I
turned away from the television and went around smelling of offal the
inedible parts of the chicken: in gardening I said excelsior:
in gardening I required no company I had to forgive my own failure
to perceive how things were between them since I was not privileged:
I went out barelegged at dusk and dug and dug and dug for a better
understanding: I hit rock my ovaries softened: in gardening I was protean
as in no other realm before or since: I longed to torch my old belongings
and belch a little flame of satisfaction: in gardening I longed to stroll
farther into soundlessness: I could almost forget what happened
many swift years ago in arkansas: I felt like a god from down under:
chthonian: in gardening I thought this is it body and soul I am home
at last: excelsior: praise the grass: in gardening I fled the fold
that supported the war: only in gardening could I stop shrieking:
stop: stop the slaughter: only in gardening could I press my ear to
the ground to hear my soul let out an unyielding noise: my lines
softened: I turned the water onto the joyfilled boychild: only
in gardening did I feel fit to partake to go on trembling in the
last light: I confess the abject urge to weed your beds while
the bittersweet overwhelmed my day lilies: I summoned the courage
to grin: I climbed the hill with my bucket and slept like a dipper in
the cool of your body besotted with growth infected by green.

John Yau

THE NEWLY RENOVATED OPERA HOUSE ON GILLIGAN'S ISLAND

Between the hastily sketched chalk curtains a backdrop of blue cliffs and avalanche mist rising toward a quarter moon. The old, bearded shepherd, who is famous for his reenactments of the early torments of bruised tots, stands up and points to the baloney stains on his shirt, each word forming like a soap bubble on the craters of his huge, cracked, blue lips. A bamboo sewing machine monitors the smell of rotten food trapped beneath the snow. Sound of a train compartment window being opened, accompanied by a foreign, possibly threatening language, gutturals mixed with sand and glass. Guided by pulleys, four ebony sticks roll two purple cabbages painted like salesmen's bruised brains down the aisle of the third class coach. A murderous scream is heard in the balcony causing the audience to turn away from the stage, which a moment later is illuminated by red searchlights. A piece of slightly charred, synthetic material, mostly white, floats to the floor. A woman, who is a weathered, wooden tower, gazes at the horizon, while the sounds of lovesick whales become increasingly louder. At first she appears diffident, but it is soon quite obvious that she has spent the past few hours sobbing into a damp hanky, which she occasionally wrings out with machine-like efficiency. A man limps onto the stage and squints up at the creaking tower. He begins a lengthy monolog of scabrous insults mixed with detailed comments about animal infidelity and the recent invasion of earth by creatures who resemble child movie stars. When he finishes, he falls to his knees and fishes two jade green marbles from his vest pocket. For the first time the woman notices him and says: You little punctured zygote. How dare you fondle your sprockets in my presence. Heed my warning or you will end your days drooling over yourself and your tarnished brood of loved ones. You will live long enough to see your grandchildren dwelling among ants, smaller than the ones that come to feed them bits of meat held between shiny black pincers.

Kneeling amidst the cool winds undulating across the stage, the man pays no attention to the woman's lava of accusations, its bubbles of ochre bombast. There are other bursts to consider, particularly since his distinctive, undersized nose has started bleeding, and he finds it impossible to staunch the apparently endless cascade. A pool of brownish liquid forms a small lake, where two women in yellow Easter bonnets are drowning. In the illuminated distance, which is separated from the lake by a stone wall built during the reign of a toothless tyrant, three slightly overweight, garrulous policemen are riding silver bicycles. The middle one is carrying a leather bag shaped like a child's head and finds it difficult to maintain his balance. I want to doze while time continues flowing through this planetary circuit I've been saddled with, its butter dish of blinking dreams. My own thoughts are surrounded by embroidered throwaway pillows, and I am little more than a kite string of withered, peony petals somersaulting across a kitchen counter. The sky mangled corpse of a doodlebug clings tenaciously to the storm window. The word "stupendous" is carefully printed in turquoise lipstick on the refrigerator's yellow enamel door. An empty quinine bottle spins across the counter and stops before reaching the stainless steel sink.

The sand shifts its vertical and horizontal parameters, the music of its grinding spheres broadcasting dented pulses to the scaly creatures hibernating on the irregularly arranged lower shelves. Two tents flatten into a tablecloth of stars once seen floating in the Southern hemisphere. A spotted brown-and-blue mongrel begins dancing on its hind legs around the town's last fountain, its disheveled pyramids of poisoned birds. Sheila has been told that a bright red tornado has carried off all the camels lined up at the Connecticut Taxi Stand, and now fears that she will never be able to find Aunt Jane, who vanished while walking from the hotel to the curio shop in search of old engravings of blind Japanese men to put above her bed. A loudspeaker begins broadcasting a slightly hoarse, porcelain-layered voice, which tells the crowd gathered by their windows that there is an iron bridge in the old city that will lead them to various forms of modern transportation, and that all the drivers and engineers will guarantee their passengers the lifelong supply of rejuvenation pills they will need after completing their reentry forms. As a final gesture of both disdain and gratitude, Sheila turns around and begins pulling up her black silk dress and adjusting her pale blue nylon stockings, while licking her lips with an abnormally large, purple tongue, which is the most visible result of her having devoured two dozen grape lollipops for breakfast. A huge wooden door closes. Mice scurry back into their holes and flies finally settle near drying food stains. The bald man behind the gray metal desk goes to the filing cabinet and pulls a jar of earthworms out of the bottom drawer. He turns and opens the closet and begins examining a mound of raincoats, each of which is made from a different colored plastic. A large, rubber hand descends from the hologram of a rainbow, which is rising out of the file cabinet's top drawer, and begins making corrections. The movements are simultaneously deft and mannered. Flames are engulfing the curtains and spreading towards the backdrop of windows and wooden shutters. The young, well-dressed man, who has been sitting in a leather chair on one side of the stage, crashes to the floor, clearly a stiff. Smoke fills the school cafeteria. Children scream and run in every direction, both disturbed and amused by the sight of their teachers being rapidly and painlessly transformed into the tarnished and chipped tourist items their parents inspect at garage sales. A horde of beggars has crawled over to the dead man and is skimming through his pockets. The leader is whistling a familiar tune that no one in the audience can name. A brand new column of crimson sunlight is being lowered through a convoy of threatening clouds. A faint breeze tingles the air, its fleshy remnants.

David Young

LULLABY FOR THE ELDERLY

Under the hum and whir of night, under the covers, deep in the bed, beyond all the calling of doves, past the great flares of love and pain, the daily bread and grind, it's warm as a pot, soft as a breast. It's the deep woods, the place where you come to a clearing, find the still pool, and slip gently into it—to bathe, to dive, to drown.

Your mother is there, under the leaves, smelling of milk, and your father is hiding among the trees. A giant hand tousles your hair, and the mouse is there with its dangerous eyes, the bear with his shimmering fur, the rivers that thunder off ledges and spill into gorges as mist.

When you wake, refreshed, murmur a blessing for those who have never returned. Say a word to the corn and the wheat, to the deer and squirrels and whistling toads, who brought you right up to the edge of the woods and let you go in on your own.

David Young

KITCHEN RUCKUS

Broth throbs on the stove. I journey into a turnip, but the saffron-threads, forlorn, summon me back. Dicing the cake, icing the carrot, while mites converse in the oatmeal. Singing with Tristan, humming with Brahms, as tomatoes collapse in their sauce. We hold these truths to be significant—that shrimp goes well with garlic, that bread is a Promised Land, that onions hymn in the nose . . .

Ghosts gather. Some wear aprons. They want to recall the taste of wine with well-sauced pasta, to savor brown sugar dissolved in espresso, lemon squeezed over smoked salmon. The tongue has a mind of its own. The chilis are biding their time. Wolves would come down from the mountains just for a pear and a nugget of goat cheese. Please saunter up to this counter and sample a ladle of beans, a morsel of duck, a slice of porcini, as the golden drizzle of sunlight dances outside on the grill.

And which is the poem, please? The butter, the knife that slides right through it? Bread rises, lamb braises. Fruit ripens steadfast in a handsome old bowl. I lick my lips. Oh tingling shadows! Such luck, to be alive!

Gary Young

I discovered a journal in the children's ward, and read, I'm a mother, my little boy has cancer. Further on, a girl has written, this is my nineteenth operation. She says, sometimes it's easier to write than to talk, and I'm so afraid. She's offered me a page in the book. My son is sleeping in the room next door. This afternoon, I held my whole weight to his body while a doctor drove needles deep into his leg. My son screamed, Daddy, they're hurting me, don't let them hurt me, make them stop. I want to write, how brave you are, but I need a little courage of my own, so I write, forgive me, I know I let them hurt you, please don't worry. If I have to, I can do it again.

Gary Young

My son is learning about death, about the possibilities. His cat was killed. Then Mark died, then Ernesto. He watched the news, and saw soldiers bulldozed into the earth after battle. Down the road, a boy his age was found floating in a pond. My son says, we're careful about water, and splashes in his own warm bath. We don't want to die, he says, we want to live forever. We only just die later, he says, and nods his head. Death is comprehensible; what comes later is a week away, or two, and never arrives.

Andrew Zawacki

INCOGNITO

It won't be long now: ice like anvils crowding the eave-spouts and
gutters, the roof hammered into corrugation. The day is darker sooner,
night's gossamer performing its service, the front yard anaesthetized,
the back yard already in coma. There are few alternatives but to sweat
like a spore among the rattling hemlocks and survey the beetles in their
glassy stasis. Begin your lament for the disappearing sun strophes, know
that what is missing is always here, wingless and parched. Renounce
the footworn ladder rung and the bent nail: the sonar will find you lean-
ing into the crimson of a near coast, or gone under, or stranded on a
chiseled peak, clinging to the serif of an unknown letter.

Gene Zeiger

THE HOLE

Today I ironed a woolen shawl which a woman in Calcutta spent six months embroidering. She sold it for a song because the buyer, my ex-husband, found three moth holes at one end. I'd never bargain with that woman, I'd never offer her fewer rupees because of a few small holes.

The hole in the shawl is the hole in the screen that lets the flies in, is the hole in the world through which people come and go, is the "luch in kup" my father ascribed to the truly dumb. The rabbit scurries into it, the snake. It is the space between the rocks through which the sheep flee, through which the world enters, shyly at first, then brazen.

The hole is the proverbial eye of the needle, the gap between the teeth, the rip through which the dead return with their old coats and hats, the sound of feet stamping to unloosen the dust.

Mend it—fill it, glut it, wet it, stitch it, paste it, stuff it with vowels, consonants, entire dictionaries, nothing works. What can you do? There's the hole! How can you fit into that tiny space gracefully, then live there with so little room?

Gene Zeiger

THE WIND

Down the early roads the fierce wind scatters dry leaves in packs; they remind me of bugs or mice racing spuriously anywhere—over the metal sap buckets that have blown off the maples, over the edge of the stubbled cornfield.

Something is wrong; it requires a rearrangement of shape, of intent, as when Laurie was dying. She asked, *remember me in the wind,* and I do: her sparest of frames, her eyes burning above the bones.

The wind has knocked out power and phone service; I can only talk to myself now—what has happened to this world? When I look out the big window, I think: *this, this is the silence you have held out for.*

James A. Zoller

SKY UPON US

(for Stefan, 8)

We don't think like this when the sky is upon us, snow thick in the air from clouds almost within reach. Then, we think of the falling, snow riding the wind over and through the trees, blinding us, or snow drifting from the sky in deep quiet as if snowfall had meaning if only we could stop, if only we could hear those minutely crashing forms.

But this morning the snow is on the ground and the sky grows deeper blue by the minute and the sun, dropping black shadows from tree and hill, strikes brilliantly across the snowscape.

We blink and haul our tube to the top of the hill, blink at the bright sun on the single packed trail to the bottom, sit one atop the other on the tube, slide quickly in the hard groove.

Together we sail over the ice, over bumps and pits; gain speed as any falling object, learn gravity, minutely aware of distance time inertia, mouths open, voices torn out and lost to the wind; sail through the run, sail into the deep snow beyond, plowing, gliding, spraying cold powder until the tube stops and we fly apart, tumble, collide.

How different this all is: this cold horizontal world, the bite of cold snow on our faces, sky like deep immaculate water, the shocks our bodies absorb and mine remembers. I roll myself over, struggle against soft snow to gain my feet; the sky blazes the snow dazzles, you scamper toward the steep path just as laughter and shouts collide in my ears and lungs, catching up.

Epilogue

Russell Edson

THE PROSE POEM AS A BEAUTIFUL ANIMAL

He had been writing a prose poem, and had succeeded in mating a giraffe with an elephant. Scientists from all over the world came to see the product: The body looked like an elephant's, but it had the neck of a giraffe with a small elephant's head and a short trunk that wiggled like a wet noodle.

You have created a beautiful new animal, said one of the scientists.

Do you really like it?

Like it? cried the scientist, I adore it, and would love to have sex with it that I might create another beautiful animal . . .

SELECTED BIBLIOGRAPHY

What follows is a selected bibliography of criticism on the prose poem. I encourage readers to send bibliographical information along with hard copies of essays that are not listed below. I thank Michel Delville for compiling the first draft of this list.

Alexander, Robert. "The American Prose Poem, 1890-1980." Dissertation, the University of Wisconsin-Milwaukee, 1982.

Beaujour, Michel. "Short Epiphanies: Two Contextual Approaches to the French Prose Poem." In Caws and Riffaterre, eds.

Benedikt, Michael. Introduction. *The Prose Poem: An International Anthology.* New York: Dell, 1976.

Bly, Robert. "What the Prose Poem Carries with IT." *The American Poetry Review* 6, no. 3 (1977).

———. "On Writing Prose Poems: An Interview with Rochelle Ratner." In *Talking All Morning.* Ann Arbor: University of Michigan Press, 1982.

———. "The Prose Poem as an Evolving Form." In *Selected Poems.* New York: Harper & Row, 1986.

Boyd, Greg. "An Application of Paradox." [pamphlet] Santa Maria: Asylum Arts, 1993.

Breuning, Leroy C. "Why France?" In Caws and Riffaterre, eds.

Brownstein, Michael. "Introduction." *The Dice Cup: Selected Poems of Max Jacob.* New York: Sun Press, 1979.

Caws, Mary Ann. "The Self-Defining Prose Poem: On Its Edge." In Caws and Riffaterre, eds.

Caws, Mary Ann, and Hermine Riffaterre, eds. *The Prose Poem in France: Theory and Practice.* New York: Columbia University Press, 1983.

Cohn, Robert G. "A Poetry-Prose Cross." In Caws and Riffaterre, eds.

Coleman, Elliot. "Poetry and Prose: The Prose Poem." *The University of Dayton Review* 2, no. 1 (1967): 7-21.

Deguy, Michel. "Poeme en prose, prose en poeme." In Caws and Riffaterre, eds.

Edson, Russell. "The Prose Poem in America." *Parnassus,* 5, no. 1 (1976): 321-5.

———. "On Counting Sheep." In *Fifty Contemporary Poets: The Creative Process.* Alberta T. Turner, ed. New York: David McKay, 1977.

———. "Portrait of the Writer as a Fat Man: Some Subjective Ideas or Notions on the Care and Feeding of Prose Poems." In a *Field Guide to Contemporary Poetry and Poetics.* Stuart Friebert and David Young, eds. New York: Longman, 1980.

———. "The Soul of Tales." Book Review. *Parnassas,* 16, no. 1.

Fredman, Stephen. *Poet's Prose: The Crisis in American Verse* [second edition]. Cambridge: Cambridge University Press, 1990.

Füger, Wilhelm. Introduction. *English Prose Lyrics: An Anthology.* Heidelberg: Carl Einter Universitätsverlag, 1976.

Gerlach, John. "The Margins of Narrative: The Very Short Story, the Prose Poem, and the Lyric." In *Short Story Theory at a Crossroads*. Susan Lohafer and Jo Ellyn Clarey, eds. Baton Rouge: Louisiana State University Press, 1989.

Holden, Jonathan. "The 'Prose Lyric'." In *The Rhetoric of the Contemporary Lyric*. Bloomington: Indiana University Press, 1989.

Horvath, Brooke. "Why the Prose Poem?" In *Denver Quarterly* 25, no. 4 (1991): 105-15.

——. "The Prose Poem and the Secret Life of Poetry." *American Poetry Review* 21, no. 5 (1992): 11-14.

Hubert, Renee R. "Characteristics of an Undefinable Genre: The Surrealist Prose Poem." *Symposium* 22 (1968): 25-34.

Ignatow, David. "An Interview: With Gerard Malanga" in *Open Between Us*, edited by Ralph J. Mills, Jr. Ann Arbor: University of Michigan Press, 1980.

Johnson, Barbara. "Disfiguring Poetic Language." In Caws and Riffaterre, eds.

Keene, Dennis, ed. Introduction. *The Modern Japanese Prose Poem*. Princeton: Princeton University Press, 1980.

Le Guin, Ursula. "Reciprocity of Prose and Poetry." In *Dancing at the Edge of the World*. New York: Grove Press, 1989.

Levertov, Denise. "What Is a Prose Poem?" *The Nation* 193, no. 22 (1961): 518-19.

Meyers, George Jr., ed. *Epiphanies: The Prose Poem Now*. Westerville: Cumberland Press, 1987.

Monroe, Jonathan. *A Poverty of Objects: The Prose Poem and the Politics of Genre*. Ithaca: Cornell University Press, 1987.

Murphy, Marguerite S. *A Tradition of Subversion: The Prose Poem in English from Wilde to Ashbery*. Amherst: University of Massachusetts Press, 1992.

Perloff, Marjorie. "Lucent and Inescapable Rhythms: Metrical 'Choice' and Historical Formation." In *The Line in Postmodern Poetry*. Robert J. Frank and Henry M. Sayre, eds. Urbana: University of Illinois Press, 1988.

Ramke, Bin. "A Gesture of Permission: On Poems in Prose, etc." *Denver Quarterly*, 25, no. 4 (1991): 129-35.

Riffaterre, Hermine. "Reading Constants: The Practice of the Prose Poem." In Caws and Riffaterre, eds.

Riffaterre, Michael. "On the Prose Poem's Formal Features." In Caws and Riffaterre, eds.

Shattuck, Roger. "Vibratory Organism: *crise de prose*." In Caws and Riffaterre, eds.

Silliman, Ron. "The New Sentence." In *Talks: Hills 6/7*. Bob Perlman, ed. San Francisco: Bob Perlman, 1980.

——. "New Prose, New Prose Poem." In *Postmodern Fiction: A Bio-Bibliographical Guide*. Larry McCaffery, ed. New York: Greenwood Press, 1986.

Simon, John. "Prose Poem." *Princeton Encyclopedia of Poetry and Poetics*.

Alex Preminger, Frank Warnke, and O. B. Hardison, eds. Princeton: Princeton University Press, 1965.

——. *The Prose Poem as a Genre in Nineteenth-Century Literature.* New York: Garland Publishing, 1987.

Sonnenfeld, Albert. "L'adieu supreme and Ultimate Composure: The Boundaries of the Prose Poem." In Caws and Riffaterre, eds.

Terdiman, Richard. "The Paradoxes of Distinction: The Prose Poem as Prose." In *Discourse/Counter/Discourse: Theory and Practice of Symbolic Resistance in Nineteenth Century France.* Ithaca: Cornell University Press, 1995.

——. "The Dialectics of the Prose Poem." Ibid.

Todorov, Tzvetan. "Poetry Without Verse." In Caws and Riffaterre, eds.

Tyler, Parker. Preface. *A Little Anthology of Poems in Prose.* Charles Henri Ford, ed. New Directions 14 (1953): 330-6.

Wesling, Donald. "Narrative of Grammar in the Prose Poem." In *The New Poetries: Poetic Form Since Coleridge and Wordsworth.* Lewisburg: Bucknell University Press, 1985.

Special Issues of Literary Journals on The Prose Poem

Madrona, Volume 2, Number 7, 1973. Edited by John Levy with an essay, "Introduction to Prose Poetry."

Pebble, Number 11, "Fifty-Four Prose Poems," July, 1974. Edited by Greg Kuzma and Duane Ackerson.

Arion's Dolphin, Volume 3, Numbers 3 and 4, Summer-Autumn, 1974. Edited by Stratis Haviaras with an introductory essay by James Randall, "Some Notes on the Prose Poem: Historical and Practical."

Indiana Review, Volume 9, Number 2, 1986. Edited by Pamela Wampler with an essay by Marianne Boruch, "Edson's Head."

Time Is Not Enough for the World, Volumes 1 and 2, 1986. Two special issues of *The Montana Review*, Vols. 8 and 9. Edited by Rich Ives. Collections of short-shorts and prose poems.

Denver Quarterly, Volume 25, Number 4, Spring 1991. Edited by Donald Revell with essays by Wayne Dodd ("And Now a Few Words"), Brooke Horvath ("Why the Prose Poem?"), Marjorie Perloff ("Lyn Hejinian's *My Life*"), and Bin Ramke ("A Gesture of Permission").

lift, Number 7, August 1991. Edited by Joseph Torra with an essay by Gian Lombardo, "My Uncle, the Monkey, Sings on Wednesdays, When He's on My Back: Some Notes on Poems-in-Prose and Prose-in-Poems."

The Illinois Review, Fall 1995/Spring 1996: Vol. 3, Nos. 1 & 2. Special double issue called "Prictions for the 21st Century." Prose poems and short-short fiction, edited by Jim Elledge.

Verse, Volume 13, Number 1. Special section on prose poetry, with an introduction by Charles Simic.

Literary Journals

Paragraph. Edited by Walker Rumble and Karen Donovan. 18 Beach Point Drive, East Providence, RI 02915. 1985-

The Prose Poem: An International Journal. Edited by Peter Johnson. English Department, Providence College, Providence, RI 02918. 1992-

Quarter After Eight. Edited by Matthew Cooperman. Ellis Hall, Ohio University, Athens, OH 45701. 1995-

key satch(el). Edited by Gian Lombardo. Quale Press, PO Box 363, Haydenville, MA 01039-0363. E-Mail: keysatch@quale.com. 1996-

Anthologies

The Prose Poem: An International Anthology. Edited with an introduction by Michael Benedikt. New York: Dell, 1976.

Imperial Messages: One Hundred Modern Parables. Edited with an introduction by Howard Schwartz. Woodstock, NY: Overlook Press, 1991.

The Anatomy of Water: A Sampling of Contemporary American Prose Poetry. Edited with an introduction by Steve Wilson. Georgia: Linwood Publishers, 1992.

A Curious Architecture: New British and American Prose Poetry. London: Stride Press, 1993.

Models of the Universe: An Anthology of The Prose Poem, edited by Stuart Friebert, David Walker, and David Young. Oberlin: Field Editions, 1995.

The Party Train: An Anthology of North American Prose Poetry, edited by C.W. Truesdale, Mark Vinz, and Robert Alexander. Minneapolis: New Rivers Press, 1995.

Suddenly: Prose Poetry and Sudden Fiction. Edited by Jackie Pelham. Houston, Texas: Martin House, 1998.

Always the Beautiful Answer: A Prose Poem Primer. Edited by Ruth Moon Kempher. St. Augustine, Florida: Kings Estate Press, 1999.

CONTRIBUTORS

Kim Addonizio is the author of three books of poetry, the most recent of which is *Tell Me* (BOA Editions); her book of stories, *In the Box Called Pleasure*, was recently published by Fiction Collective 2.

Robert Alexander is the author of a book of prose poems, *White Pine Sucker River: Poems 1970-1990*, and he has co-edited two anthologies, *The Party Train: A Collection of North American Prose Poetry* and *The Talking Hands: A Thirtieth Anniversary Celebration*. All three books are available from New Rivers Press. He is currently working on a narrative prose poem about the Civil War battle of Five Forks.

Agha Shahid Ali is Director of the M.F.A. Creative Writing Program at the University of Massachusetts-Amherst. His latest collections are *A Nostalgist's Map of America* and *The Country Without a Post Office*.

Jack Anderson, a poet and dance critic, received the Marie Alexander Award for his *Traffic: New and Selected Prose Poems* (New Rivers Press).

Nin Andrews is the author of *The Book of Orgasms* and *Spontaneous Breasts*.

Rane Arroyo is a Puerto Rican poet and playwright who is widely published and performed. He is the son of Jean Genet and Emily Dickinson–with Pablo Neruda as the Holy Ghost.

Rose Ausländer was born in what is now Romania and wrote in German. Of Jewish origin, she survived WWII and immigrated to the United States in 1946, where she worked for the next seventeen years as a secretary, correspondent and translator. She returned to Europe in 1963, and died in Düsseldorf, Germany in 1988. Her first volume of poetry was published in 1939; her second in 1965. These translations are reprinted by permission of S. Fischer Verlag and Gary Sea. Copyright © 1984 S. Fischer Verlag GmbHm Frankfurt an Main.

Ruth Behar's poems are included in three new anthologies: *Sephardic American Voices: Two Hundred Years of a Literary Legacy* (Brandeis University Press, 1996); *Little Havana Blues: A Cuban-American Literature Anthology* (Arte Publico Press, 1996); and *The Prairie Schooner Anthology of Jewish-American Writers*, edited by Hilda Raz (Lincoln: University of Nebraska Press, 1998). The poem included in this volume forms part of a manuscript entitled *Nameless Poems/Poemas sin nombre*, which explores the themes of love, loss, and regret, as well as Behar's search for bonds to Cuba, her place of birth.

Michael Benedikt has published five books of poetry, including *Mole Notes, Night Cries*, and *The Badminton at Great Barrington*. He also edited the *Poetry of Surrealism* and *The Prose Poem: An International Anthology*. His new manuscript of prose poems is called *Universe.*

Aloysius Bertrand (1807-1841) has sometimes been called "The Father of the Modern Prose Poem," though he never used the term to describe his own work. The poem in this volume is from *The Fantasies of Gaspard de la Nuit*, a book Baudelaire cited as the precursor to his *Paris Spleen.*

Robert Bly's latest books of poetry include *Eating the Honey of Words: New and Selected Poems* (Harper Collins) and *The Lightning Should Have Fallen on Ghalib: Selected Poems of Ghalib*, Ecco Press, translated with Sunil Dutta. He also edited *The Best American Poetry* 1999 (Scribner).

Michael Bowden lives in Sierra Vista, Arizona. His prose poems have appeared sporadically in various journals over the years, and have been included in two anthologies: *Fever Dreams: Contemporary Arizona Poetry* and *The Party Train: A Collection of North American Prose Poetry.*

John Bradley lives with his wife, Jana, in DeKalb, where he teaches writing at Northern Illinois University. An essay of his on the prose poem appeared in *Quarter After Eight.*

Joel Brouwer, a 1999-2000 NEA fellow, is the author of *Exactly What Happened* (Purdue, 1999). "Tumor" and "Marked" are from a manuscript of 100-word prose poems, *Centuries*, which is currently seeking a publisher.

Christopher Buckley's ninth book of poetry, *Fall From Grace,* was recently published by BkMk Press/University of Missouri, Kansas City. With Gary Young he has just edited *The Geography of Home: California and the Poetry of Place* (Hey Day Books, 1999). He is Chair of the Creative Writing Dept. at the University of California/Riverside.

Lynne Burris Butler won the 1999 Blue Lynx Poetry Prize for her collection of poems *Sunday Afternoons with Tolstoy*. She teaches at the University of North Alabama.

George Chambers, novelist and poet, teaches at Bradley University. He is the author of *The Bonnyclabber* (novel), *Null Set* (short stories), and *The Last Man Standing* (novel). According to Ray Federman, he and Chambers "have been writing together—sending the stuff back and forth, until we feel it's in place. I think we are on to something—a series of sorts."

Maxine Chernoff has published five books of poems and five collections of fiction, most recently her novel, *A Boy in Winter* (Crown).

Michael Chitwood is the author of three collections of poetry: *Salt Works, Whet* and *The Weave Room*. He also has a book of essays titled *Hitting Below the Bible Belt*.

David Citino is Professor of English and Creative Writing at Ohio State University. He is the author of ten books of poetry, including *The Book of Appassionata: Collected Poems* (Ohio State University Press); also *Broken Symmetry* (Ohio State), named a Notable Book of 1997 by the National Book Critics Circle; *The Weight of the Heart* (Quarterly Review of Literature Poetry Series, 1996); *The Discipline: New and Selected Poems*, 1980-1992 (Ohio State); *The Appassionata Doctrines* (Cleveland State University Poetry Center); and *The Gift of Fire* (University of Arkansas Press).

Killarney Clary is the author of two collections of poetry: *Who Whispered Near Me* (Farrar, Straus and Giroux, 1989) and *By Common Salt* (Oberlin College Press, 1993). She was a 1992 Lannan Foundation Fellowship recipient.

Mark Cunningham received an MFA in creative writing from the University of Virginia a few years ago. He's stayed in the area because it's close to Washington D.C., where most museums don't charge to get in.

Craig Czury's most recent books are *Unreconciled Faces* (Foot Hills Publishing, 1999) and *Parallel Rivertime* (bilingual Russian/English edition Petropol Press, St. Petersburg, Russia, 1999). He lives in Reading, Pennsylvania where he conducts his ongoing Berks Poetry Project with the African-American, Hispanic, Asian and Anglo communities.

Philip Dacey's latest books are *The Deathbed Playboy* (Eastern Washington University Press, 1999) and *The Paramour of the Moving Air* (Quarterly Review of Literature, 1999).

Jon Davis's latest book is *Scrimmage of Appetite* (University of Akron Press, 1995).

Aleš Debeljak's recent books in English include *Reluctant Modernity: Institution of Art and its Historical Forms* and *The City and the Child*. He lives in Ljubljana, Slovenia.

Michel Delville teaches twentieth-century British and American literature at the University of Liège, Belgium. His published works include a study of J. G. Ballard (Northcote House, 1998) and articles on contemporary poetry and fiction. His book, *The American Prose Poem: Poetic Form and the Boundaries of Genre* (University Press of Florida, 1998), won the 1998 SAMLA Studies Award.

Chard deNiord is the author of *Asleep in the Fire,* published in 1990 by the University of Alabama Press. His poems have appeared recently in *The Push-cart Prize XXII 1998, Best American Poetry, 1999, Ploughshares, The New England Review,* and *Agni.* He teaches English and Creative Writing at Providence College.

Peter Desy. Bored with central Ohio, Desy is settling in northern California. He has poems recently in *America, Willow Review, key satch(el),* and *Illuminations.*

Ray DiPalma is the author of more than thirty-five collections of poetry and graphic works. His books include: *Numbers and Tempers, Provocations, Motion of the Cypher,* and most recently, *Letters.*

Liljana Dirjan ranks among Macedonia's most important younger poets. In 1985, she received the Macedonian national book award for her second book, *Live Measure,* during the same festival at which Yannis Ritsos received the international award for poetry.

Stuart Dybek is the author of a collection of poems, *Brass Knuckles,* and two collections of stories. His chapbook of short prose, *The Story of Mist,* was published by The State Street Press.

Russell Edson's most recent book is *The Tunnel: Selected Poems,* from Oberlin College Press.

Nikos Engonopoulos (1907-1985) was the *enfant terrible* of Greek Surrealism. "Maria of the Night" is from his first book, *Do Not Speak to the Driver* (1938).

Elke Erb lives in what used to be East Berlin. She has edited many anthologies and translated Gogal, Blok and other Russian writers. Two of her books have appeared with West German publishers: *Einer schreit: Nicht!* and *Trost.*

Clayton Eshleman's most recent collection of poetry is *From Scratch* (Black Sparrow Press, 1998). Talon Books (Vancouver) will publish *Companion Spider,* a large collection of his essays and interviews, in 2000.

Raymond Federman is a bilingual novelist, poet, translator, critic, and author of seven novels (the latest *To Whom It May Concern*), and three volumes of poems (the latest *Now Then*). Distinguished Professor at SUNY Buffalo, he teaches creative writing in the English Department.

Gary Fincke's newest book is *The Almanac for Desire* (BkMk Press, 2000). New poems are in *The Paris Review, Doubletake, American Scholar,* and *The Iowa Review.*

Lawrence Fixel lives in San Francisco. His most recent publication was the limited edition chapbook, *Lost Subjects/Found Objects: Poems 1945/1998.*

Charles Fort is Reynolds Chair in Poetry and Professor of English at University of Nebraska at Kearney. A MacDowell Fellow, he has received major awards from the Poetry Society of America, Writer's Voice, and the Randall Jarrell Poetry Prize. He has published work in sixteen anthologies. Fort's books include: *The Town Clock Burning* (Carnegie Mellon University Press, under the Classic Contemporary Series) and *Darvil* (St. Andrews Press); *We Did Not Fear The Father* and *As The Lilac Burned The Laurel Grew* are both Reynolds Chair Books.

Richard Garcia's poems have recently appeared in *The Colorado Review*, *Crab Orchard Review*, and *Luna*. His next book, *Rancho Notorious*, is forthcoming from BOA Editions. He is poet-in-residence at Children's Hospital in Los Angeles.

Val Gerstle's work has appeared in over forty publications, including *Cincinnati Poetry Review*, *Bellingham Review*, and *Louisville Review*. She has an MFA in Creative Writing from Bowling Green State University, and she teaches at Northern Kentucky University.

Amy Gerstler is a writer living in Los Angeles. Her most recent book of poetry is *Crown of Weeds*. *Medicine,* a book of her poems, will be published by Penguin Putnam in 2000.

Gary Gildner's most recent books are *The Birthday Party* (Limberlost, 2000) and *The Bunker in the Parsley Fields* (Iowa, 1997), which received the Iowa Poetry Prize. He lives in the Clearwater Mountains of Idaho.

James Vladimir Gill was a gifted poet, novelist, and essayist, and former editor and founder of the influential international literary journal *2PLUS2*. He also one of the early contributing editors of this journal. We will always miss his intelligence and kindness.

Ray Gonzalez is the author of five books of poetry, including *Cabato Sentora* and *The Heat of Arrivals,* both from BOA Editions. In 2000, the University of Arizona Press will publish *Turtle Pictures,* a poetic/prose cultural memoir, which contains a number of prose poems. He is the editor of twelve anthologies, has served as a Poetry Editor of *The Bloomsbury Review* for eighteen years, and recently founded a new poetry journal, *Luna*. He was recently appointed McKnight Land Grant Professor at the University of Minnesota.

Miriam Goodman's *Expense Report* won the 1995 Warm Springs Press Chapbook competition and appeared in summer 1995. Her newest collection, *Commercial Traveller*, was published in 1996 by Garden Street Press. She teaches a class in word and image at the Radcliffe Seminars and makes her living as a digital instructional designer.

David Greenslade lives in Wales where he publishes in Welsh and English. English language books include *Welsh Fever,* a look at Welsh immigrant life in the U.S.A. Prose poetry collections include *Cambrian Country*, a study of Welsh Emblems, and *Creosote*, an investigation of the vegetable soul.

Richard Gwyn's most recent book is a collection of forty-two prose poems, *Walking on Bones* (Parthian Books). After several years living in Greece and Spain he now lives in Cardiff where he works as a lecturer and researcher in health communication.

Leo Haber, adjunct professor of Hebrew at Union College, N.Y., and consulting editor at *Midstream,* has published poetry and fiction in a wide variety of journals including *Commentary*, *Midstream*, *The Literary Review*, *River City*, *Southern Poetry Review*, *Snake Nation Review*, *Voices West*, and *The Prose Poem: An International Journal*. Mr. Haber has won awards in poetry from Embers, Poetpourri, Rome Art and Community Center, and the Poetry Society of Dallas, Texas. Two of his poems appeared in an international anthology of Holocaust poetry, *Beyond Lament*, edited by Marguerite M. Striar and published by Northwestern University Press in 1998.

S.C. Hahn lives on a farm near Falköping in southern Sweden, where he is milking cows, translating Swedish and German poetry, and writing a novel about the Nebraska Territory.

Cecil Helman was born in 1944 in Cape Town, South Africa, but now resides in London. He previously published in journals and anthologies, including, *The Prose Poem: An International Anthology* (ed. Michael Benedikt, Dell, 1976), and *Imperial Messages: One Hundred Modern Parables* (ed. Howard Schwartz, Avon, 1976). Books include: *The Body of Frankenstein's Monster: Essays in Myth and Medicine* (W. W. Norton, 1992).

Bob Heman has spent the last twenty years working in libraries and archives. His prose poems have appeared in numerous journals including *Caliban*, *Artful Dodge*, *First Intensity*, *Yefief* and *key satch(el)*.

Brian Henry's first book of poetry, *Astronaut*, appeared in 1999 from Arc in the U.K.

Jennifer L. Holley received her M.F.A. from the School of the Art Institute of Chicago. She lives in Old Saybrook, Connecticut, and works for the *Yale Alumni Magazine.*

Brooke Horvath is the author of two collections of poetry: *In a Neighborhood of Dying Light* and *Consolation at Ground Zero.* A Professor of English at Kent State University and editor with the *Review of Contemporary Fiction,* his recent work includes co-edited books on William Goyen, George Garrett, Thomas Pynchon, and Henry James.

Holly Iglesias' work has appeared in journals including *The Massachusetts Review, Cream City Review, Puerto del Sol, Kalliope* and *The Women's Review of Books.* In 1999, she completed a dissertation, *Boxing Inside the Box: Women's Prose Poetry;* and her chapbook, *All That Echoes Her Large,* was published by Permafrost. She is co-editor, with Catherine Reid, of *Every Woman I've Ever Loved: Lesbian Writers on Their Mothers* (Cleis Press, 1997).

David Ignatow's *Against the Evidence: Selected Poems 1934-94* © Wesleyan University Press. His recent death was a great loss to the poetry community and to *The Prose Poem: An International Journal.* As a contributing editor, his kindness and good humor were a continual source of encouragement.

Maria Jacketti's first collection of poetry, *Black Diamond Madonna,* is forthcoming from Cross Cultural Communications. She is currently translating Neruda's *Cantos Ceremoniales* and *Maremoto.*

Gray Jacobik is the 1998 winner of the X. J. Kennedy Poetry Prize; her book, *The Surface of Last Scattering* is out from Texas Review Press. *The Double Task,* published by University of Massachusetts Press, received the Juniper Prize for 1997. Recent poems appear in *The Kenyon Review, Poetry, Alaska Quarterly Review,* and *Best American Poetry 1999.*

Sibyl James' books include *The Adventures of Stout Mama* and *In China with Harpo and Karl.* She has taught in the U.S., China, Mexico, and as Fulbright professor in Tunisia and Côte d'Ivoire.

Louis Jenkins lives in Duluth, Minnesota. His most recent book of prose poems is *Just Above Water* (Holy Cow! Press, 1997). Two of his prose poems were published in *The Best American Poetry 1999.* He is currently working with visual artist Richard C. Johnson on a project titled *The Third Image: Words and Pictures.*

Brian Johnson's poems have appeared in *American Letters and Commentary, Connecticut Review, North Dakota Quarterly, Quarter after Eight* and other journals. His chapbook, *Self-Portrait,* is forthcoming from Quale Press.

Jim Johnson lives in Duluth, Minnesota. His most recent book is *Dovetailed Corners* (Holy Cow! Press).

Peter Johnson is founder and editor of *The Prose Poem: An International Journal*. His latest books of prose poetry are *Pretty Happy!* (White Pine Press, 1997) and *Love Poems for the Millennium* (Quale Press, 1998). He received an NEA for Creative Writing in 1999.

George Kalamaras' poems and prose poems appear in many places, including *Best American Poetry 1997*, *Epoch*, *The Iowa Review*, *TriQuarterly*, and elsewhere. His collection of poetry, *The Theory and Function of Mangoes,* won the Four Way Books Intro Series in Poetry Award (Published March 2000).

Paol Keineg is a Breton poet who lives in the U.S. Recent books are *Tohu* (Wigman, 1994) and *Silva rerum* (Guernica/Nadeau, 1989). He is currently working on a play.

Bill Knott's latest books are *Other Strangers Than Our Own: Selected Love Poems, 1963-1999*; *Homages*; *The Season on our Sleeve: Short Poems, Selected Poems, Volume One, 1968-88*; and *Plaza de Loco: New Poems 1999*.

Mary A. Koncel's chapbook, *Closer to Day*, was published by Quale Press.

Stephen Kuusisto is the author of a memoir, *Planet of the Blind.* His first collection of poems, *Night Seasons*, will soon be available from Copper Canyon Press. He is a graduate of the "Writers' Workshop" at the University of Iowa.

David Lazar's work has appeared in *The Anchor Essay Annual: Best of 1998*, *Chelsea*, *Southwest Review*, *Denver Quarterly* and other journals and magazines. He has four citations for "Notable Essays of the Year" from *Best American Essays*. He edited *Conversations for M.F.K. Fisher* and *Michael Powell: Interviews* for University Press of Mississippi, and he is a member of the creative writing faculty at Ohio University.

Sydney Lea, founding editor of *New England Review*, has held fellowships from the Guggenheim, Rockefeller and Fulbright Foundations. He is author of six books of poetry, the latest of which, *To The Bone*, won the 1998 Poets' Prize. His new collection, *Pursuit of a Wound*, will appear next year. He has also published a novel and a collection of naturalist essays. The translations in this issue are forthcoming in an anthology of Henri Michaux's work edited by the poet Nin Andrews.

David Lehman translated some of the prose poems of Henri Michaux when he (Lehman) divided a graduate year between Cambridge University and Paris in the early 1970s. He has recently returned to the task. His latest book of nonfiction is *The Last Avant-Garde: The Making of the New York School of Poets (1998)*, which will appear as a Doubleday Anchor paperback in fall 1999. His new book of poems, *The Daily Mirror*, will be published by Scribner in January 2000.

Larry Levis: At the time of his death in May 1996, Larry Levis was Professor of English at Virginia Commonwealth University in Richmond, VA. He published five collections of poetry during his life and his posthumous book *Elegy* was published by the University of Pittsburgh Press in 1997. A *Selected Poems* is forthcoming, also from the University of Pittsburgh Press. His honors included the U.S. Award of the International Poetry Forum, a Lamont Prize, a selection for the National Poetry Series, grants from the Guggenheim, NEA, Virginia Commission for the Arts, and a Fulbright award. Levis was one of the most unique and significant poetic talents of the past fifty years.

P. H. Liotta's most recent books include *The Nightingale Is Among Us Again: Selected Poems from the Macedonian of Bogomil Gjuzel*; *The Ruins of Athens: A Balkan Memoir*; and *Dismembering the State: The Logic and Ill-Logic of Yugoslav Disintegration*. His manuscript of prose poems, currently circulating, is called *The Blue Whale*.

Rachel Loden's collection *Hotel Imperium* won the Contemporary Poetry Series competition of the University of Georgia Press and was published in fall 1999. Her chapbook, *The Last Campaign*, won the Hudson Valley Writers' Center competition, and her poems have appeared in the *Paris Review, Antioch Review, New American Writing, Best American Poetry 1995*, and elsewhere.

Gian Lombardo's most recent prose poetry collections are *Who Lets Go First* (Swamp Press, 1999) and *Sky Open Again* (Dolphin-Moon, 1997).

Robert Hill Long is a Carolinian who endures a mild western Oregon exile. He has been a fellow of the NEA, the North Carolina Arts Council, and the Oregon Arts Commission. His books include *The Power to Die, The Work of the Bow*, and *The Effigies*. His work has appeared in *Best American Poetry, Flash Fiction* and journals in every direction: from *Poetry East* to *Poetry Northwest, New England Review* to *Southern Poetry Review*, and lots of points in between.

Dennis Maloney is a poet, translator, and landscape architect. In addition, he is the editor of the widely respected White Pine Press. His books of translation include *The Stones of Chile* by Pablo Neruda; *The Landscape Of Soria* by Antonio Machado; *Dusk Lingers*, Haiku of Issa; and *Tangled Hair, Love Poems of Yosano Akiko* (with Hide Oshiro). Several volumes of his own poems have been published, including *The Map Is Not the Territory* (Unicorn Press, 1990).

Morton Marcus' latest book of prose poems, *When People Could Fly*, was published by Hanging Loose in 1997. His new and selected prose poems, *Moments Without Names*, has been selected to be part of the Marie Alexander Series of New Rivers Press and will be out next year.

Peter Markus has published prose poems and short-short fictions in *Black Warrior Review, Quarterly West, Quarter After Eight, Barnabe Mountain Review*, and *Third Coast*, as well as in the anthology *The Party Train: A Collection of North American Prose Poetry,* published by New Rivers Press.

Dionisio D. Martínez was born in Cuba and is the author of *Climbing Back* (forthcoming from Norton, 2000), selected for the National Poetry Series by Jorie Graham; *Bad Alchemy* (Norton, 1995); and *History as a Second Language* (Ohio State, 1993). He has received fellowships from the Guggenheim Foundation, the National Endowment for the Arts, and the Whiting Foundation. He lives in Tampa, Florida.

Michael Martone has written five books of short prose. The most recent is *Seeing Eye*, published by Zoland Books in 1995. He lives in Tuscaloosa, Alabama.

William Matthews died on November 12, 1997. He published ten collections of poetry, including *Blues If You Want* (1989), *Selected Poems & Translations, 1969-1991* (1992), and *Time and Money* (1995). He received the 1997 Ruth Lilly Poetry Prize. His prose poems in this volume are from his second collection, *Sleek for the Long Flight*, which was reprinted by White Pine Press and is still available.

Kathleen McGookey has poems published recently in *Epoch, Bellingham Review, Seneca Review, Salt Hill, Boston Review,* and *Verse*. Her first collection, *Whatever Shines*, will be published by New Rivers Press in the spring of 2001.

Martin McKinsey has published his own poetry in such journals as *Ploughshares* and *Webster Review*, and his translations of Greek poets have appeared widely. He is the translator of *Late Into the Night: The Last Poems of Yannis Ritsos* (Oberlin, 1995), and he is also the author of *Point Taenaron* (Tapir, 1997), a book of poems.

Jay Meek has published seven books with Carnegie Mellon, including *Windows*, a collection of prose poems, and *The Memphis Letters*, a sequence of fictional letters, available this year. Last spring, on leave from the University of North Dakota, he completed a new collection of prose poems in Norway.

Christopher Merrill's recent books include *Only the Nails Remain: Scenes from the Balkan Wars* (nonfiction) and the translation of Aleš Debeljak's *The City and the Child.*

Henri Michaux (1899-1984) was one of the early geniuses of the prose poem, whose intellectual and playful sensibility continues to inspire a new generation of prose poets.

Gabriela Mistral was the only Latin American woman to receive the Nobel Prize for literature. After receiving the prize, she suggested she had won because she was the "candidate of the women and children." She died in New York City in 1957. Her prose poems are from *Gabriela Mistral: A Reader,* available from White Pine Press.

Fred Muratori's two poetry collections are *Despite Repeated Warnings* (BASFAL Books, 1994) and *The Possible* (State Street Press, 1988). His poems have appeared in *The Best American Poetry 1994, New American Writing, Poetry International,* and many other journals. He lives just outside Ithaca, New York.

Pablo Neruda was born in the frontier lands of southern Chile in 1904. At an early age, he began a life of charged political and poetic activity. In 1971, Neruda, often referred to as "the poet of enslaved humanity," was awarded the Nobel Prize for Literature. Neruda died in Santiago, Chile in 1973. "The Key" is from *The House in the Sand* (Milkweed, 1990).

Kristy Nielsen has published work in *Mid-American Review, The Madison Review, Kalliope,* and *Spoon River Poetry Review,* among others. Her work was included in *The Party Train: A Collection of North American Prose Poetry* (New Rivers) and a chapbook of prose poems, *Two Girls,* is available from Thorngate Road.

Naomi Shihab Nye's recent books include *Fuel* (poems), *Habibi* (a novel for teens), and *Lullaby Raft* (a picture book).

Nina Nyhart has two collections of poems from Alice James Books, *Openers* and *French for Soldiers.* Her prose poems have appeared in *Amaranth, Fine Madness, Green Fuse, Sing Heavenly Muse!, The Snail's Pace Review, Sojourner, Tampa Review, Whole Notes,* and in *The Party Train: An Anthology of North American Prose Poetry,* New Rivers Press, 1996.

Tommy Olofsson is a Swedish poet and a translator; he is also a critic for the Swedish Daily newspaper *Svenska Dagbladet.* "Chicago" is from *Elemental Poems* (White Pine Press, 1989).

Imre Oravecz has published five books of poetry, most recently, *September 1972,* a book which sold out overnight in Hungary. Translations of his work appeared in Volume 1 of this journal.

Jean Pearson is a poet and writer from Bethlehem, Pennsylvania. Her most recent book of poems is *On Speaking Terms With the Earth.*

Robert Perchan's book is *Perchan's Chorea.* He is currently at work on a long prose-poem sequence called *Essence & Senescence & Miss Kim.*

Jane Lunin Perel is professor of English and Women's Studies at Providence College. She has published four collections of verse poetry. She has just discovered prose poetry.

Francis (Martínez de) Picabia (1879-1953), an avant-garde Parisian artist of Cuban extraction, was a champion of the various 20th-century "isms," and helped to introduce Dadaism into the USA in 1915. As a writer, his linguistic nihilism is exemplified in several collections, especially *Jésus-Christ rastaquouère* (1920), in which the present "entr'acte" appears, with little apparent relation to the rest of the work.

Cristian Popescu (1959-95) published three books, almost entirely prose poetry, including the chapbook *The Popescu Family* (1987) and *The Popescu Art* (1994). His works have appeared in English in the U.S. in Adam Sorkin's co-translations in *Green Mountains Review*, *Poetry Daily*, *Brevity* and in Romania in *Apostrof* and in the anthology, *Romanian Poets of the 80s and 90s* (*Paralela* 45, 1999).

Constance Pultz grew up in New York State and lives in Charleston, South Carolina. The Nobel Prize committee has never heard of her two chapbooks.

Jacques Réda was born in Lunéville in 1929. In 1940 he moved to within striking distance of Paris, and thirteen years later he found himself there for good. His many works include *Les Ruines de Paris* (1977), *Retour au calme* (1989), and *Lettre sur l'univers* (1991). The selections here are from *The Ruins of Paris* (Reaktion Books: London).

Pierre Reverdy (1889-1960) is a major representative of the French surrealist prose poem. "Combat Area" and "Behind the Eyelids" are from *La balle au bond,* a collection first published in 1928 and still unavailable in English translation.

Yannis Ritsos (1909-1990) was one of the foremost poets of modern Greece. A collection of his prose writing, *Iconostasis of Anonymous Saints*, is available from Kedros Editions.

Vern Rutsala has published many books of poetry, including a book of prose poems, titled *Little-Known Sports*, which won the Juniper Prize in 1994.

Gary Sea is a member of the American Literary Translator Association. He has published translations from German and Modern Greek in various journals, most recently in *Asylum, Confluence, Graham House Review, Nimrod*, and *Webster Review*.

Norman Shapiro has published *Selected Poems from Baudelaire's "Les Fleurs du mal"* and *A Hundred and One Poems of Paul Verlaine* (both at the University of Chicago Press); poems in *Partisan Review* and *The Formalist*; a couple of short pieces in both *Beacons* (the ATA literary journal) and *Two Voices*.

John Shoemaker is a writer, editor and musician who lives in Seattle, Washington.

Barry Silesky is the author of *One Thing That Can Save Us*, prose poems (called short-short fiction by Coffee House Press); a collection of verse; and poems in many magazines and anthologies. He has also authored the biography of Lawrence Ferlinghetti, edits the magazine *ACM*, and is at work on the biography of John Gardner, for Algonquin Books.

Charles Simic is a poet, essayist and translator. He has published fourteen collections of his own poetry, five books of essays and memoirs, and numerous books of translations. His new book of poems, *Jackstraws*, was published in spring of 1999 by Harcourt Brace.

Goran Simić is the author of *Sprinting from the Graveyard*, translated by David Harsent. He lives in Toronto.

William Slaughter is a professor of English at the University of North Florida. He has been a senior Fulbright Lecturer in China (1987-88) and Egypt (1980-81). He is the author of *The Politics of My Heart* (1996), a book of poems and essays, and *Untold Stories* (1990), a book of poems. He edits and publishes *Mudlark*, an electronic journal of poetry and poetics. His poems and essays have appeared in magazines ranging from *Poetry* (Chicago) to *Exquisite Corpse*.

Bruce Smith teaches in the writing program at the University of Alabama. His previous collections of poetry are *The Common Wages, Silver and Information* (National Poetry Series Selection), *Mercy Seat* and, most recently, *The Other Lover* (University of Chicago).

Ellen McGrath Smith is a Ph.D. candidate in literature at Duquesne University, where she is completing a doctoral dissertation that deals with the American prose poem. She received the M.F.A. in poetry degree from the University of Pittsburgh and continues to teach community and academic poetry workshops in the Pittsburgh area.

Thomas R. Smith's third book of poems, *The Dark Indigo Current*, was published this year by Holy Cow! Press. His work is included in *The Best American Poetry 1999* (Scribner).

Linda Smukler, winner of the 1997 Firecracker Alternative Book Award in Poetry, is the author of two collections of poetry: *Normal Sex* and *Home in Three Days. Don't Wash.*, a multi-media project with accompanying cd-rom. Smukler has received fellowships in poetry from the New York Foundation for the Arts and the Astraea Foundation.

Adam J. Sorkin published three single-author volumes of Romanian poetry during the past year: Daniela Crăsnaru's *Sea-Level Zero* from BOA, selected poems largely translated with the poet; Ioana Ieronnim's *The Triumph of the Water Witch,* from Bloodaxe, a volume of prose poems translated with the poet; and Mircea Cărtărescu's *Bebop Baby* in the *Poetry New York* pamphlet series.

Maura Stanton's fourth book of poetry, *Life Among the Trolls*, was published by Carnegie Mellon in 1998. She teaches at Indiana University in Bloomington.

Borgan Stefănescu is on the faculty of the University of Bucharest; in 1996-97, he was Fulbright lecturer at Penn State. A translator and essayist, his co-translations with Adam Sorkin of Cristian Popescu, Marin Sorescu, and others have appeared in half a dozen magazines and anthologies.

J. David Stevens has published poems and stories in *The Paris Review*, *The Iowa Review*, *The North American Review*, and *The Virginia Quarterly Review*, among others. He currently teaches creative writing at Seton Hall University.

Brian Swann has published many books. He teaches at the Cooper Union.

Jean Tardieu is one of the leading voices in France today. Since 1933 his plays, poems, essays and other texts have been published by Gallimard. His most recent works are *On vient chercher monsieur Jean* and *La Comédie de la comédie*, both with Gallimard, 1990.

James Tate's most recent book is *Shroud of the Gnome*, Ecco Press, 1997.

Carine Topal lives, writes, and teaches in Los Angeles. She is the recipient of several poetry awards and the author of *God As Thief*, her first collection of poems, published by The Amagansett Press.

Helen Tzagoloff has recently been published in *Riverrun*, *The MacGuffin*, *Anthology of Magazine Verse & Yearbook of American Poetry*, and other journals. She has completed a poetry manuscript, *Eye Contact*.

Mark Vinz is the author of several collections, including a book of prose poems, *Late Night Calls*. He is also co-editor of *The Party Train: A Collection of North American Prose Poetry*, published by New Rivers Press.

Chris Volpe teaches a poetry workshop at the University of New Hampshire. His recent work has appeared in *New American Writing*, *The New Republic* and *The Antioch Review*.

Diane Wald's new book, *Lucid Suitcase*, is available from Red Hen Press. Her electronic chapbook, *Improvisations on Titles of Works by Jean Dubuffet*, can be seen on the *Mudlark* website.

Liz Waldner's first book is *Homing Devices* (O Books, 1998); her second, which won a 1999 Iowa Prize for Poetry, is *A Point Is That Which Has No Part* (University of Iowa Press, 2000). *With the Tongues of Angels* (Green Lake Chapbook Prize) is also due in 2000.

Rosmarie Waldrop's recent books of poems are *Reluctant Gravities* (New Directions, 1999), *Split Infinites* (Singing Horse Press, 1998), and *Another Language: Selected Poems* (Talisman House, 1997).

Charles Harper Webb has won the Morse Poetry Prize, the Kate Tufts Discovery Award, and a Whiting Writer's Award. His latest book, *Liver*, won the 1999 Felix Pollak Prize and was published by the University of Wisconsin Press.

Tom Whalen teaches creative writing, literature, and film, and divides his time between New Orleans and Germany. His latest books are *Roithamer's Universe* (a novel), *Winter Coat* (poetry), and, with Daniel Quinn, the comic fiction *A Newcomer's Guide to the Afterlife*.

M. L. Williams' work has appeared in numerous magazines and anthologies, including *The Geography of Home, Verse and Universe: Poems about Mathematics and Science, What There Is: The Crossroads Anthology, Solo, The Prose Poem*, and *Quarterly West*. He is currently at work on two anthologies, *The Obsessive Refrain: French Forms in Contemporary American Verse* with co-editor Chryss Yost, and a new anthology of Fresno poets with David Oliveira. He currently lives in Santa Barbara, California.

Peter Wortsman is the author of a short collection of prose, *A Modern Way To Die* (Fromm International, 1991, paperback 1993) and translator of, among other works, *Posthumous Papers of a Living Author*, by Robert Musil (reissued by Penguin Twentieth Century Classics in 1996).

C.D. Wright's latest books are *Tremble* and *Deepstep Come Shining*.

John Yau has a book of essays forthcoming from the University of Michigan Press. His most recent books include *Forbidden Entries* (1996) and *My Symptoms* (1998).

David Young has published eight books of poetry, one of them, *Work Lights*, made up entirely of prose poems. His interest in the prose poem is also reflected in the anthology he co-edited, with Stuart Friebert, *Models of the Universe* (Oberlin College Press).

Gary Young's most recent books are *Days* and *Braver Deeds*, which won the Peregrine Smith Poetry Prize. He edits the Greenhouse Review Press and his print work is represented in many collections including the Museum of Modern Art and the Getty Center for the Arts.

Andrew Zawacki is co-editor of *Verse* and he reviews for the *TLS*. His poems have appeared in *New American Writing, The New Republic, Boston Review, Denver Quarterly, Colorado Review* and elsewhere.

Gene Zeiger lives in western Massachusetts and is the author of two collections of poetry, *Sudden Dancing* (Amherst Writers and Artists Press) and *Leaving Egypt* (White Pine Press). Her memoir, *How I Find Her*, is forthcoming.

Clark M. Zlotchew, a professor of Spanish at the SUNY College at Fredonia, is a writer and translator. He is the author of *Libido into Literature: The "Primera Epoca" of Galdos,* published by Borgo in 1990, and of *Voices of the River Plate: Interviews with Writers of Argentina and Uruguay*, from Borgo in 1991.

James A. Zoller teaches at Houghton College in Houghton, New York, and has published widely.

Quarterly West

Poetry • Fiction • Creative Nonfiction • Reviews

Quarterly West

Twentieth Anniversary
Issue

Ai	Rodney Jones	Maurya Simon
Agha Shahid Ali	Allison Joseph	Sherod Santos
David Baker	Philip Levine	Gary Soto
Jeanne Marie Beaumont	Larry Levis	Nance Van Winckel
Christopher Buckley	William Matthews	Gordon Weaver
Fred Chappell	Beauvais McCaddon	Charles Harper Webb
Alan Cheuse	Lynne McMahon	Bruce Weigl
H. E. Francis	Antonya Nelson	David Wojahn
Patricia Goedicke	Lucia Perillo	Robert Wrigley
Albert Goldbarth	Jan Ramjerdi	Paul Zimmer
T. R. Hummer	Bin Ramke	

★ *Pushcart Prize: 1996, 1998, 2000* ★ *Best American Short Stories: 1996* ★
★ *Best American Poetry: 1997, 2000* ★ *New Stories from the South: 1997, 1998* ★

Sponsors of a biennial novella competition since 1982.

Quarterly West

SUBSCRIPTIONS:
1 year (2 issues) $12.00
2 years (4 issues) $21.00
Single issues $7.50

Quarterly West
University of Utah
200 S Central Campus Dr, Rm 317
Salt Lake City UT 84112-9109

EPOCH

FICTION, POETRY, ESSAYS SINCE 1947

Painting, "Monument with Kerbstones," 1991 by Camille Ward. Oil on paper 14" x 16"

Published three times per year. Sample copy $5.00. One year subscription $11.00.

Available from 251 Goldwin Smith Hall, Cornell University, Ithaca, NY 14853

VERSE

IN OUR NEXT ISSUE (15.3):

AUSTRALIAN POETRY FEATURE

POEMS by Javant Biarujia, Peter Boyle, Pam Brown, Stephen Edgar, Kevin Hart, Kris Hemensley, S.K. Kelen, John Kinsella, Emma Lew, Peter Minter, Peter Porter, Peter Rose, Gig Ryan,Tracy Ryan, Andrew Sant, John Tranter, Toby Wallace, Chris Wallace-Crabbe, Ania Walwicz, Lucy Wilks, and others.

ESSAYS by Peter Boyle on Charles Wright, Kevin Hart on Mark Strand, and Peter Rose on Wallace Stevens.

INTERVIEWS with John Kinsella and others.

REVIEWS: Judith Bishop on Sarah Day, Emma Lew, Rhyll McMaster, Fay Zwicky; Graham Foust on John Tranter; John Kinsella on John Forbes; Adam Kirsch on Anthony Lawrence; Peg Peoples on Pam Brown; Margot Schilpp on Philip Salom; Susan Schultz on Gig Ryan; Mark Wallace on John Kinsella; David Wheatley on Chris Wallace-Crabbe; David McCooey on Australian poetry anthologies; and others.

PLUS:

POEMS by Jonathan Monroe, Peter Richards, Matthew Rohrer, Susan Schultz, Karen Volkman, David Wheatley, and others.

INTERVIEWS with Tomaz Salamun and David Constantine.

ESSAY: Matthew Zapruder on Anna Swir and Liliana Ursu.

REVIEWS: Selina Guinness on Ted Hughes; David Yezzi on Amy Clampitt; Margaret Hermes on Marianne Moore's letters; Tony Brown on August Kleinzahler; Emily Taylor on Peter Reading; Ray Gonzalez on Gary Soto, Juan Felipe Herrera, Victor Hernandez Cruz; Matthew Zapruder on Larry Levis; Preston Merchant on James Lasdun; Justin Quinn on Peter Fallon; Sinead Garrigan on David Wheatley; Mike Theune on Olena Kalytiak Davis.

UNTITLED

a magazine of prose poetry
presents its premier issue
featuring writing by:

Laynie Browne
Paul Naylor
Dan Featherston
Spencer Selby
Rupert Loydell
John Olson
Tosa Motokiyu
Craig Watson
Ray Ragosta
Sheila E. Murphy
Jono Schneider
Leonard Brink

Elke Erb
Keith Waldrop
Rosmarie Waldrop
Gad Hollander
Dennis Phillips
Ethan Paquin
Andrew Felsinger
Sarah Rosenthal
Peter Johnson
Gian Lombardo
Francis Raven
& others…

Single copy price: **$8**
Subscription to issues #1 and #2: **$12**

Please make checks payable to: · Leonard Brink
Instress Press
P.O. Box 3124
Saratoga, CA 95070

www.poetrypress.com

$500 PRIZE

Could this be you?

The spring 2001 Mississippi Review will celebrate the 400th anniversary of *Hamlet* with a special issue conceived and edited by David Berry. A $500 prize will go to the "best of the issue." There is no reading fee.

We urge the discovery and contribution of parodies, newly unearthed soliloquies, cartoons, letters between (or addressed to) the characters, short stories, prose poems, plays, and other material fitted to the *Hamlet* universe. The editor is also interested in critical articles, but only as authored by poets, playwrights, or fiction writers, please (Hamlet being all three).

Send submissions to David3Berry@aol.com or to 306 Washington Ave., Ocean Springs, MS 39564. Postmark deadline isOctober 27, 2000.

Quale Press is sorry to announce that it is no longer publishing
the magazine *key satch(el)*. However, in its stead, Quale Press is
pleased to announce *edition key satch(el)*, a quarterly series of
prose poetry chapbooks that starts publishing in early 2000.

Subscriptions: *Print version* — single copy price $5.00;
$16.00/year (4 chapbooks); $30.00/two years (8 chapbooks);
outside U.S. please add $9.00 per year for postage.
Electronic version — single copy price $3.00; $10.00/year
(4 chapbooks); $18.00/two years (8 chapbooks).

edition key satch(el), Quale Press, P.O. Box 363,
Haydenville, MA 01039-0363. keysatch@quale.com.
www.quale.com/ks/kshome.html

ISSN: 1527-9579

Individual chapbooks distributed by
Small Press Distribution, 1341 Seventh St., Berkeley, CA 94710

EDITION

$\mathbf{K}$ey
$\mathbf{S}$atch(el)